CONTEMPORARY TOPICS 3

ADVANCED LISTENING AND NOTE-TAKING SKILLS

SECOND EDITION

DAVID BEGLAR

NEIL MURRAY

MICHAEL ROST
SERIES EDITOR

longman.com

Contemporary Topics 3: Advanced Listening and Note-Taking Skills
Second Edition

Pearson Education, 10 Bank Street, White Plains, NY 10606

Vice president, publishing: Allen Ascher
Editorial director: Louisa Hellegers
Acquisitions editor: Eleanor Barnes
Development director: Penny Laporte
Development editor: Lise Minovitz
Vice president, director of design and production: Rhea Banker
Executive managing editor: Linda Moser
Production manager: Ray Keating
Associate production editor: Melissa Leyva
Director of manufacturing: Patrice Fraccio
Senior manufacturing buyer: Dave Dickey
Photo research: Tara Maldonado
Cover design: Elizabeth Carlson
Cover image: Artville.com
Text design: Debbie Iverson
Text composition: Color Associates
Text art: Color Associates

Photo credits: **1** left: Getty Images, Inc./ Photo Disc, Inc.; center: © 2001 Photo disc; right: © Corbis Stock Market; **8** © Corbis Stock Market; **16** © Corbis Stock Market/ Ariel Skelley; **23** left: © Corbis Stock Market/ Rob Lewine; right: © Corbis Stock Market/ George Shelley; **31** left: © Esbin/ Anderson/ Omni-Photo Communications, Inc.; right: Eleanor Kirby Barnes; **39** Getty Images, Inc.; **46** Anthro-Photo File/ Terrace; **53** © Michelle Bridwell/ PhotoEdit; **61** © Corbis Stock Market/ Nadine Markova; **69** left: (Picasso) Getty Images, Inc.; center: (Michael Jordan) © Duomo/ William R. Sallaz, Duomo Photography Ltd.; right: (Mozart) Bildarchiv der Oesterreichische Nationalbibliothek; **78** Corbis Digital Stock; **87** © Sanford Kossin.

Text credits: **30** excerpted with permission from "The Price Collector," by Robert Brenner, Brenner Information Group (http://www.brennerbooks.com); **85** excerpted with permission from Survival International (www.survival-international.org), a worldwide organization supporting tribal peoples.

All dictionary definitions checked by Longman lexicographers.

Library of Congress Cataloging-in-Publication Data

Beglar, David.
Contemporary topics 3--advanced listening and note-taking skills / David Beglar, Neil Murray.-- 2nd ed.
p. cm. -- (Contemporary topics series)
Rev. ed of: Contemporary topics--advanced listening comprehension.
ISBN 0-13-094862-4
I. Title: Contemporary topics three--advanced listening and note-taking skills. II. Title: Advanced listening and note-taking skills. III. Murray, Neil (Neil L.) IV. Beglar, David. Contemporary topics--advanced listening comprehension. V. Title. VI. Series.
PE1128.B419 2002
428.3'4--dc21

2002016186

ISBN 0-13-094862-4

Printed in the United States of America
4 5 6 7 8 9 10–BAH–05 04 03

CONTENTS

Scope and Sequence

Unit	Topic	Note-Taking Tip
1 Slang: Talking *Cool*	Communication Studies	Organize main ideas and supporting details
2 Murphy's Law	Statistics	Note numbers and statistics
3 Types of Memory	Cognitive Science	List and number items
4 Actions Speak Louder than Words	Psychology	Use abbreviations and symbols
5 Marriage: Traditions and Trends	Sociology	Make charts
6 Black Holes, White Holes, and Wormholes	Astronomy	Draw sketches
7 Animal Talk	Cognitive Linguistics	Note Descriptions
8 Gender Differences in Language	Language and Communication	Note comparisons and contrasts
9 Fashion and Status	Fashion Design	Note definitions
10 The Making of Genius	Behavioral Science	Note processes
11 The New Global Superculture	Sociology	Note examples
12 Computer Security	Computer Science	Note causes and effects

Corpus-Based Vocabulary	Projects
decade / deviates / exploit / persist with / phenomenon / priority	Discussing slang Listening for slang in movies
anticipate / device / encounter / random / revolution / widespread	Discussing Murphy's Law Reading about probability theory
conceivable / distorted / duration / phenomena / somewhat / temporarily / visual	Presenting memorization techniques Researching ways to improve memory
bulk / clarification / differentiate / dynamic / integral / intensity / minimal	Demonstrating gestures Discussing body language in business
conform / erode / mature / norm / obligations / subordinate / undergoing	Ranking marriage partner characteristics Presenting marriage customs
ceased / collapse / controversial / deny / empirical / identical / via	Discussing time travel Researching astronomy
confirm / contrary / innovation / manipulate / rigid / straightforward / tranquil	Conducting interviews about pets Writing a response to an article
contemporary / crucial / devoted to / dramatic / exhibit / inherent	Evaluating the lecturer's conclusions Analyzing male/female conversation styles
abandoned / conform / definite / hierarchical / radical / vehicles	Giving a presentation Summarizing an article
detect / enormous / intense / notwithstanding / persistence / quoted	Ranking advice Examining multiple intelligences
commodities / diminishing / highlighted / homogeneous/ ideologies / inevitable / insight	Discussing symbols of global culture Reading about endangered cultures
colleague / detect / integrity / persist / scenarios / via	Conducting interviews about computer security Researching computer crime

Acknowledgments

The series editor, authors, and publisher would like to thank the following consultants, reviewers, and teachers who offered invaluable insights and suggestions for the second edition of the *Contemporary Topics* series: Michele Alvarez, *University of Miami;* Dorothy Avondstrondt, *University of Miami;* Cynthia Bermudez, *University of Miami;* Ana Maria Bradley Hess, *Miami-Dade Community College;* David Burger, *Seigakuin University;* David Chatham, *Osaka YMCA International College;* Mary Erickson, *Wichita State University;* Heidi Evans, *Wisconsin English as a Second Language Institute;* Carole Franklin, *University of Houston;* Charlotte Gilman, *Texas Intensive English Program;* Talin Grigorian, *American English Institute;* Aaron Grow, *Pierce College, Washington;* Adele Hanson, *University of Minnesota;* Patty Heiser, *University of Washington;* Funda Jasanu, *Yeditepe University, Istanbul, Turkey;* Greg Jewell, *Drexel University;* Lorne Kirkwold, *Hokkai Gakuen University;* Oswaldo Lopez, *Miami-Dade Community College;* Diane Mahin, *University of Miami;* Michele McMenamin, *Rutgers University;* Donna McVey, *Drexel University;* Masanori Nishi, *Osaka YMCA International College;* Patrick O'Brien, *Hokkai Gakuen University;* Gary Ockey, *International University of Japan;* Bivin Poole, *Osaka YMCA International College;* Kathy Sherak, *San Francisco State University;* Eiji Suenaga, *Hokkai Gakuen University;* Margaret Teske, *Mount San Antonio College;* Bill Thomas, *Wichita State University;* Margery Toll, *California State University at Fresno;* James Vance, *ELS Language Center, St. Joseph's University;* Susan Vik, *Boston University;* Andrea Voitus, *California State University at Fresno;* Cheryl Wecksler, *Drexel University;* and Jean Wilson, *Toyo Eiwa University.*

In addition, the authors of *Contemporary Topics 3* would like to thank Eleanor Barnes, Lise Minovitz, and Michael Rost for their enormous support during the writing of *Contemporary Topics 3.* Their perceptive and incisive feedback on the material was invaluable, and their professionalism was crucial to maintaining the momentum of the project and bringing it to fruition. We would also like to thank Averil Coxhead for allowing us the use of the *Academic Word List.* Thanks also go to Faye and Alexander Murray for helping create computer graphics for concepts mentioned in the book, and to all those who took the time to provide us with their ideas about how we might improve the first edition of *Contemporary Topics 3.*

Preface to the *Contemporary Topics* Series, Second Edition

As many language teachers now realize, listening is not simply an important skill. It is also essential for progress in language learning. Effective listening enhances students' abilities to pay attention, remember new grammar and vocabulary, process ideas, and respond appropriately. As students develop their listening abilities, they feel more capable and confident in all aspects of language use.

Students at different levels need different kinds of listening skills and strategies, but most eventually encounter the need for academic listening. More than merely enabling them to succeed in college lectures and discussions, effective academic listening allows students to build, synthesize, and use knowledge in the target language. As a result, they can fully participate in the exchange of authentic ideas about relevant topics.

Recent progress in language teaching and testing has provided many new instructional approaches and strategies that help students develop good academic listening skills. *Contemporary Topics*, a three-level audio and text series, incorporates these new ideas into a coherent, carefully sequenced approach that works well in a variety of classrooms.

Authentic Language and Active Listening

Each level of the series comprises twelve original lectures on relevant contemporary topics drawn from a range of academic disciplines that are accessible to students of all backgrounds. In a feature new to this edition, the lectures are recorded in an interactive style that models both the natural, authentic language of academic lectures and the active listening of students questioning and responding to the teacher. In addition, the lectures include explicit discourse markers that guide understanding. Key points are also reinforced so that they are easier to remember.

The activities that accompany each lecture are designed to slow down the listening process. Students are encouraged to preview vocabulary, listen with a clear purpose, take notes efficiently, organize and review their notes, and apply the content. The activities also help students develop critical thinking skills, including:

- activating prior knowledge
- guessing meaning from context
- predicting information
- organizing ideas
- discriminating between main ideas and details
- reconstructing and summarizing main ideas
- transferring knowledge from lectures to other areas

The Academic Word List

Because *Contemporary Topics* is designed as a bridge to the world of content listening, at least half the target vocabulary in each lecture is drawn from the latest academic word corpora. The Academic Word List in Appendix A, developed by Averil Coxhead, consists of ten sublists containing the most commonly used academic vocabulary. Of these lists, Sublist 1 contains the most frequently used words, Sublist 2 the next most frequently used, and so on. *Contemporary Topics 1* includes words from Sublists 1–4, *Contemporary Topics 2* includes words from Sublists 5–7, and *Contemporary Topics 3* includes words from Sublists 7–10. As students progress through the series, they internalize the vocabulary they need to understand academic lectures on a wide range of topics.

In addition to the Academic Word List, the Affix Charts in Appendix B provide a useful tool for building academic vocabulary.

Although the lectures and activities in this series provide the basis for learning, the key to making *Contemporary Topics* work in the classroom is involvement. Listening is an active process that involves predicting, guessing, interacting, risk-taking, clarifying, questioning, and responding. The authors and editors of *Contemporary Topics* have created a rich framework for making students more active, successful learners and teachers more active guides in that process.

Michael Rost, Ph.D.
Series Editor

Introduction

We had several goals in revising *Contemporary Topics 3.* As with the first edition, we wanted to find a way to make lectures interesting, lively, and sometimes humorous—and appropriate for students at an advanced level. Our search led us to select from a wide range of academic topics and to record lectures in as authentic a style as possible, with student interaction and natural language. In developing the accompanying student activities, we rediscovered many fundamental principles of successful learning:

- Students need to be actively involved in each stage of the lesson.
- Students need to develop an underlying knowledge of words and concepts that will help them comprehend new ideas and make inferences.
- Students need opportunities to revise their study skills.
- Students need the expectation of a clear outcome to focus their efforts.

This book and audio program is the result of our efforts to find "the right stuff"—the right content and the right learning activities—to engage students in the classroom and prepare them for the more challenging learning experiences of an academic environment. We also wanted to make the learning stages in each unit as transparent as possible, so sections are clearly labeled and activities are clearly ordered.

Organization of Units

The Student Book consists of twelve units. Although the units are sequenced, they can stand on their own. Each unit contains six sections: Topic Preview, Vocabulary Preview, Taking Better Notes, Listening to the Lecture, Using Your Notes, and Projects.

Topic Preview Each unit opens with a title and one or more pictures. By spending a few minutes talking about the pictures, students begin to predict what will be covered in the lecture. The Topic Preview questions can be answered in pairs or small groups. This section introduces the topic, stimulates interest, and elicits background knowledge and vocabulary related to the topic.

Vocabulary Preview The Vocabulary Preview prepares students by previewing academic vocabulary specific to the lecture they will hear. First, students try to guess the meanings of common academic words. Then they read dictionary entries for more technical lecture-specific vocabulary. Finally, they check the pronunciation of the new words by consulting a dictionary.

Taking Better Notes Recent research has underlined the importance of effective note-taking as a strategy for effective listening. In this edition of *Contemporary Topics 3,* we present specific note-taking strategies before students listen to the lecture and provide students an opportunity to practice the strategy in a brief controlled activity. As a result, students are better prepared to take good notes as they listen to the lecture itself.

Listening to the Lecture In this section, students begin by making predictions about the lecture content based on the earlier activities. After listening to the lecture once and taking notes on the main ideas, they use their notes to answer general questions about the lecture. While listening to the lecture a second time, they focus on understanding supporting details and correcting initial errors in their notes. Then they answer a series of questions that ask for more detailed information. The explicit requirement to use lecture notes to answer questions further underlines the importance of good note-taking.

Using Your Notes This new feature in *Contemporary Topics 3* encourages students to evaluate how well they have applied the note-taking strategies presented in Taking Better Notes. Students work with their own notes and with those of their classmates to check for specific information. In addition, they evaluate their use of the cumulative Note-Taking Tips presented throughout the textbook and discuss how they can improve their note-taking skills. Finally, they use their notes to summarize or reconstruct the lecture.

Projects This brief, practical section provides a range of projects that allow students to extend the ideas they have encountered in the lecture. Typical activities include discussion, further reading, research, interviews, and writing.

Other Components An audio program (available on both cassette and CD) accompanies this textbook. It contains recorded lectures and quizzes. A Teacher's Manual contains quizzes, lecture and quiz audioscripts, and answers to selected exercises.

To the Student

When you begin studying English in an academic environment, you will listen to lectures that require you to understand long passages of spoken English. At first, you may feel overwhelmed by the speed and content level of these lectures, especially if you have had little listening practice in your previous English courses.

There is no mystery in learning to listen to and understand lectures—but you can make it easier. Good listening skills and note-taking strategies will help you a lot. This book is designed to develop these strategies, which include predicting content, focusing on main ideas, taking good notes, and reviewing those notes effectively.

Another key to academic success is building your vocabulary. This book suggests many strategies for vocabulary-building. The Academic Word List and Affix Charts at the end of this book can give you a strong foundation in common academic vocabulary. Using both a dictionary and a thesaurus will also help.

Overall, we have designed this book to help you build the listening and note-taking skills you need. We hope you will find it engaging, and we wish you success!

David Beglar
Neil Murray

UNIT 1

Communication Studies

Slang: Talking *Cool*

Topic Preview

Work in small groups. Discuss the questions below.

1. What does the slang expression *cool* mean?
2. Look at the pictures. Describe the people. Do you think any of them are cool? If so, which ones? Why?
3. Do you know any other slang expressions? If so, what are they?

Vocabulary Preview

A The boldfaced words below are from a lecture on slang. Read each sentence. Circle the letter of the word or phrase that is closest in meaning to the boldfaced word.

1. People in business or politics often ***exploit*** language to gain power or status.
   a. completely ignore
   b. take advantage of
   c. make up
2. In interviews, people usually use ***mainstream*** language instead of slang.
   a. widely accepted
   b. very formal
   c. very informal
3. Some English teachers think learning slang is not a ***priority***. They prefer to teach standard English.
   a. easy thing
   b. difficult thing
   c. important thing
4. Language changes from ***decade*** to ***decade***. Many expressions that were fashionable in the 1950s were out of style in the 1960s.
   a. period of 100 years
   b. period of 20 years
   c. period of 10 years
5. The two people were close friends, so they used ***colloquial*** language.
   a. informal
   b. standard
   c. formal
6. The teacher couldn't ***tolerate*** the student's bad language, so he ordered her to leave the room.
   a. understand
   b. accept
   c. argue
7. Slang is not accepted in all situations because it ***deviates*** from standard, more formal expressions.
   a. differs from
   b. is the same as
   c. comes from
8. Even today, very conservative people often ***persist with*** the idea that slang is unacceptable in all situations, even informal ones.
   a. disagree entirely with
   b. continue to feel strongly about
   c. ignore the importance of

9. We ***construct*** our own style of speaking based on what we've heard throughout our lives.
   a. build
   b. desire
   c. discover

10. In some societies, language is ***associated with*** social class and education. People judge one's level in society by the kind of language used.
    a. connected to
    b. separated from
    c. not allowed by

11. The use of language is a complex ***phenomenon.*** Linguists, sociologists, anthropologists, and psychologists are all trying to understand it better.
    a. belief
    b. technique
    c. event

12. Many slang expressions that are acceptable in informal situations are ***taboo*** in more formal contexts.
    a. well known
    b. not allowed
    c. desirable

B The words below are also from the lecture. Read their definitions and the example phrases or sentences.

code-switching /ˈkoʊdˌswɪtʃɪŋ/ *n* switching from one language, or variety of language, to another one in the same conversation, especially by people who are able to speak both languages equally well

discourse /ˈdɪskɔrs/ *n* the language used in particular kinds of speech or writing: *the restraints of diplomatic discourse*

street talk /ˈstrit ˌtɔk/ *n* very informal spoken language that includes new and sometimes offensive words, and that is used especially only by people who belong to a particular group.

subculture /ˈsʌbˌkʌltʃɚ/ *n* the behavior, beliefs, activities, etc. of a particular group of people in a society that are different from the rest of the society: *the drug subculture*

underground culture /ˈʌndɚˌgraʊnd ˈkʌltʃɚ/ *n* underground music, literature, art, etc. that is not officially approved and usually seems strange or shocking: *an underground newspaper*

youth-speak /ˈyuθˌspik/ *n* informal language which is used especially by young people

C Use a dictionary to check the pronunciation of the new words in Parts A and B.

Taking Better Notes

Organizing Main Ideas and Supporting Details

There are two main purposes for taking lecture notes:

- to help you concentrate
- to record information that you can review later

Taking organized notes is very important, especially for the purpose of review. It can be helpful to write the main topics on the left side of the page. Indent the main ideas slightly to the right, and indent the supporting facts, details, and examples even farther to the right. Look at the example below.

British and American English Are Converging
—U.S. soldiers stationed in U.K. during World War II
—Influence of the media
—TV

Differences Still Exist Between U.S. & U.K. English
— U.K. speech varies with social class
— U.K. uses more moderate language than U.S.
—"really good" (U.K.) but "awesome" (U.S.)

Work with a partner. Think of one more fact, detail, or example that is relevant to the example notes, and decide where it would best fit. Explain the reasons for your choice.

When you listen to the lecture, try to take organized notes.

Listening to the Lecture

Before You Listen

You will hear a lecture about slang. Write two topics you think the speaker might discuss.

1. ______________________________

2. ______________________________

Listening for Main Ideas

A Close your book. Listen to the lecture and take notes.

B Use your notes to complete the sentences below. Circle a, b, or c.

1. The speaker defines slang as ____________.
   - a. informal language used by a particular group of people
   - b. informal language used by most people
   - c. informal language used only by young people
2. Students use slang ____________.
   - a. all the time
   - b. only where it's accepted
   - c. only in class or at work
3. Slang is considered cool because ____________. (*Circle two reasons.*)
   - a. it shows that the speaker is in style
   - b. it shows that the speaker is intelligent
   - c. it reinforces relationships
4. The most common slang theme is ____________.
   - a. love and romance
   - b. approval and disapproval
   - c. study and the workplace
5. Today, slang is ____________ it was ten years ago.
   - a. more acceptable than
   - b. less acceptable than
   - c. about as acceptable as
6. Historically, slang has been associated with ____________.
   - a. the media
   - b. youth
   - c. criminals

Listening for Details

A Close your book. Listen to the lecture again. Add supporting details to your notes and correct any mistakes.

B Use your notes to decide if the statements below are true or false. Write T (true) or F (false). Correct the false statements.

_____ 1. All cultures contain subcultures.

_____ 2. Young men and women use different slang expressions.

_____ **3.** Slang can communicate shared emotional experiences.

_____ **4.** Slang is rarely humorous.

_____ **5.** A word that "works hard" has several meanings.

_____ **6.** Many slang expressions show approval or disapproval.

_____ **7.** *Gimme five* is a slang expression that disappeared quickly.

_____ **8.** Students use more slang than colloquial vocabulary.

Using Your Notes

A Information is missing from the notes below. Use your notes to complete them.

3 Types of Slang Words

Type 1: ______________________

Examples: ______________________

chill out

____

— often terms of approval/disapproval

—some "work hard"—used often with many meanings

Type 2: ______________________

Examples: ______________________

____

____

Type 3: Words that disappear

Examples: gimme five

— often associated with personalities that come and go

B **Take notes carefully because you may not look at them again for weeks, or even months. When you look at them again, you should be able to reconstruct the lecture, or describe it in detail.**

Work in small groups. Try to use the notes from Part A to reconstruct the lecture.

C **Look at the Note-Taking Tip below. How can you improve your notes the next time you listen to a lecture?**

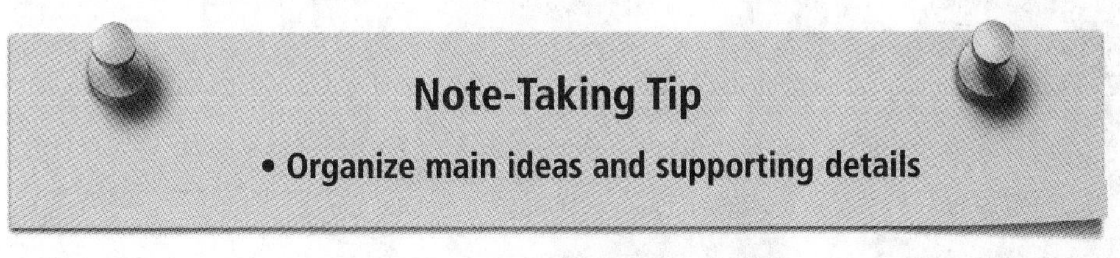

D **Rewrite or revise your notes so that the organization is clear. If you need to, listen to the lecture again.**

Projects

1. The slang expressions below were mentioned in the lecture. Discuss their possible meanings in small groups.

   wasted, chill out, hella, kick it, sweet
   the bomb, what's up, tight, bad, the man

2. Write at least five slang expressions from your culture. Then write their English definitions. Share the expressions and definitions with your classmates. Are any expressions or definitions similar? If so, which ones?

3. Read an article from an English-language magazine or the Internet. Underline any slang expressions you find. Share the expressions with your classmates and discuss their possible meanings.

4. Watch a fifteen-minute excerpt from a situation comedy or movie. Listen for slang expressions and write them down. Discuss their possible meanings.

UNIT 2

Murphy's Law

Murphy's Law: If anything can go wrong, it will.

Topic Preview

Work in small groups. Discuss the questions below.

1. What is happening in the picture? Has anything like this ever happened to you? To anyone you know? Explain.
2. According to Murphy's Law, *If anything can go wrong, it will.* What does this mean? Do you agree with this law? Why or why not?
3. Do you believe "bad luck" really exists? Why or why not?

Vocabulary Preview

A The boldfaced words below are from a lecture on Murphy's Law. Read each sentence. Guess the meanings of the boldfaced words. Compare your answers in small groups.

1. Before performing the experiment, the researcher tried to ***anticipate*** any problems that might occur.
2. People may ***perceive*** choosing the slowest line at the supermarket as bad luck, but actually luck has nothing to do with it.
3. As a car increases speed, the tires require less time to make one complete ***revolution.***
4. The ***probability*** of winning the lottery is extremely low because so many people buy tickets.
5. Most events are not ***random***; they are part of a larger pattern or plan.
6. It was a ***catastrophe*** when Ned lost all his money gambling; he had no money left for food or rent.
7. People often ***encounter*** bad luck when gambling. They may lose a lot of money before they win anything.
8. The idea that there is good and bad luck is ***widespread.*** Every culture seems to have its own particular superstitions.
9. Scientists say the blooming of a flower has a ***life history*** because a beginning, middle, and end point can be clearly identified.
10. Alice's ***theory*** is that she will win the lottery if she always plays the same numbers.
11. Some students who think ***fundamental*** arithmetic is easy have difficulty understanding more complex areas of mathematics, such as statistics.
12. A slot machine is a gambling ***device.*** If you put a coin in the machine and three identical pictures appear, you get more money back.

B **The words below are also from the lecture. Read their definitions and the example phrases and sentences.**

dice / daɪs / *n, plural* small blocks of wood or plastic with a different number of spots on each side, used in games: *Jeannie **rolled the dice**.*

fallacy / 'fæ ləsi / *n, plural* **fallacies** a false idea or belief, especially one that a lot of people believe is true: *Don't believe the fallacy that money brings happiness.*

force of gravity / ˌfɔrs əv 'grævəṯi / *n* TECHNICAL the force that makes objects fall to the ground

physics / 'fɪzɪks / *n* the science that deals with the study of physical objects and substances, and natural forces such as light, heat, movement, etc.

rate of spin / ˌreɪtəv'spɪn / *n* how quickly something spins

statistician / ˌstæṯəs'tɪʃən / *n* someone who works with STATISTICS / stə'tɪstɪks/

C **Use a dictionary to check the pronunciation of the new words in Parts A and B.**

Taking Better Notes

Noting Numbers and Statistics

Whether you are studying social sciences or physical sciences, you will often work with numbers and statistics. In order to hear numbers correctly, you need to recognize three things.

First, you need to recognize *stressed syllables*, since many numbers sound similar but have different patterns. For example:

15—fif*teen* 50—*fif*ty 19—nine*teen* 90—*nine*ty

Second, you need to listen carefully for *number group markers.* Listen for markers such as *millions, thousands,* and *hundreds.* For example:

25,678—twenty-five *thousand,* six *hundred* and seventy-eight

142,590—one hundred and forty-two *thousand,* five *hundred* and ninety

4,064,150—four *million,* sixty-four *thousand,* one *hundred* and fifty

18,244,876—eighteen *million,* two hundred and forty-four *thousand,* eight *hundred* and seventy-six

Third, you need to listen carefully for decimals, fractions, powers, and square roots. Note how they are written below.

Decimals: 2.5—two point five 0.02—point zero two (OR point oh two)

Fractions: $\frac{1}{5}$—one fifth (OR a fifth) $\frac{7}{8}$—seven eighths $2\frac{1}{3}$—two and one third (OR two and a third)

$\frac{1}{2}$—one half (OR a half) $\frac{1}{3}$—one third (OR a third) $\frac{1}{4}$—one quarter (OR a quarter)

Powers: 3^2—three squared 12^3—twelve to the third power (OR twelve cubed)

Square roots: $\sqrt{36}$—the square root of 36 $\sqrt{49}$—the square root of 49

Make a list of ten numbers. Include large numbers, decimals, fractions, powers, and square roots. Then work with a partner. Student A, read your list of numbers. Student B, take notes. Compare the list with the notes. Then change roles.

When you listen to a lecture, try to write any important numbers and statistics you hear.

Listening to the Lecture

Before You Listen

You will hear a lecture about Murphy's Law. Check (✓) two topics you think the speaker might discuss.

_____ **1.** Murphy's life history

_____ **2.** Laws about gambling

_____ **3.** Laws about statistics

_____ **4.** Computer use in statistics

_____ **5.** Predicting weather

Listening for Main Ideas

A **Close your book. Listen to the lecture and take notes.**

B **Use your notes to answer the questions below. Check (✓) a, b, or c.**

1. What has the greatest effect on whether toast falls buttered side down?

_____ **a.** the rate of spin

_____ **b.** the weight of the toast

_____ **c.** the flat shape of toast

2. What has the greatest effect on one's ability to choose the fastest supermarket line?

_____ **a.** the number of people in each line

_____ **b.** the number of lines

_____ **c.** the speed of the sales clerk

3. What is the belief that devices such as dice have a life history?

_____ **a.** probability theory

_____ **b.** single event probability

_____ **c.** the gambler's fallacy

4. Why can't statisticians predict single event probabilities?

_____ **a.** The mathematics are very complicated.

_____ **b.** There are too many uncontrolled variables.

_____ **c.** The events have no life history.

5. What is the main idea of the entire lecture?

_____ **a.** Murphy's Law is usually a form of bad luck.

_____ **b.** Murphy's Law is often based on scientific principles.

_____ **c.** Murphy's Law is often not true.

Listening for Details

A **Close your book. Listen to the lecture again. Add supporting details to your notes and correct any mistakes.**

B **Use your notes to decide if the statements below are true or false. Write T (true) or F (false). Correct the false statements.**

_____ **1.** There is a 50 percent chance that toast will land buttered-side up.

_____ **2.** The rate of spin of toast allows it to make one revolution (360° turn) before it hits the ground.

_____ **3.** The rate of spin is controlled by the force of gravity.

_____ **4.** You can use probability theory to predict whether you have chosen the fastest supermarket line.

_____ **5.** Weather patterns do not have a life history.

_____ **6.** Statisticians believe that single event probabilities cannot be calculated mathematically.

_____ **7.** Some "bad luck" has a scientific explanation.

Using Your Notes

A **Work with a partner. Exchange notes. Ask your partner questions about the numbers and statistics in his or her notes. For example:**

A: What does 50 percent refer to?

B: Some people believe toast will land buttered-side down 50 percent of the time.

Discuss how to improve the use of numbers and statistics in your notes.

B **Look at the Note-Taking Tips below. Did you use any of them when you took notes? How can you improve your notes the next time you listen to the lecture?**

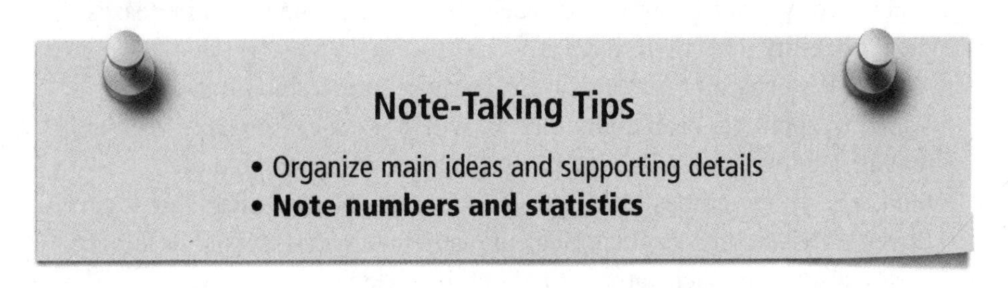

C **Rewrite or revise your notes so that all of the numbers and statistics are clear. If you need to, listen to the lecture again.**

D **Use your notes to write a summary of the lecture.**

Projects

1. Since Murphy's Law was introduced, many similar laws have been created. For example:

   Murphy's Technology Law #16: To err is human, but to really foul things up requires a computer.

   George's Law: Tell people there are 300 billion stars in the universe, and they'll believe you. Tell them a bench has wet paint on it, and they'll touch it to be sure.

   Oliver's Law: Experience is something you don't get until after you need it.

   Discuss these laws. Do you agree with any of them? Why or why not? Give examples from your experience.

2. Read the article about probability. Then answer the questions that follow.

Probability

Probability is a highly controversial concept among statisticians. One general definition is that probability is the likelihood that a particular event will occur. The values for statistical probability range from 0 (never) to 1.0 (always). For example, the probability that a person drawing a card at random from a deck of fifty-two playing cards will select a red card is 26/52, or 50 percent. The probability of drawing a diamond is 13/52, or 25 percent. Although this type of probability is straightforward, other types of probability are more complicated. Conditional probability concerns situations in which the probability of one event depends on another event. For instance, you can get sunburned without going to the beach, but going to the beach increases the probability that it will happen.

We generally use probability to make guesses about the future. We think about the probability that we will work overtime next week or that a friend will call us on the phone. When we do this type of thinking, we sometimes use Bayesian inference. Named after Thomas Bayes, an eighteenth-century English mathematician, Bayesian inference involves working backward from effect to cause by using new information to revise our estimates of probability that were based on old information. For instance, imagine that you ask a friend to go out to eat occasionally. Sometimes your friend says "yes" and sometimes "no." Your friend's answer is the effect and you are interested in the cause. After hearing "yes" and "no" a number of times, you are able to work backward and realize that there is a pattern—your friend usually says "no" at the beginning of the week (Monday or Tuesday) and usually says "yes" late in the week (Thursday or Friday). This knowledge allows you to begin making predictions about the probability of whether your friend can go out on a particular night. As you gain more experience, you may notice that the pattern is more complicated—your friend almost always says "no" on any day in the last week of the month. Thus, more information and experience allow you to judge the probability of a "yes" answer more and more accurately.

a. What is *conditional probability*?

b. What example of conditional probability is given in the article?

c. Can you think of any other examples of conditional probability? If so, what are they?

d. What is *Bayesian inference*?

e. What example of Bayesian inference is given in the article?

f. Can you think of any other examples of Bayesian inference? If so, what are they?

3. Interview someone about an experience in which he or she seemed to have bad luck. Write about the experience in detail. Try to explain what went wrong.

UNIT 3

Cognitive Science

Types of Memory

Topic Preview

Work in small groups. Discuss the questions below.

1. Look at the picture. Do you think memory is important for this person? Why or why not?
2. At what other times is a good memory important?
3. Do you think memory is important for learning vocabulary? Why or why not?
4. Rank the following techniques for remembering vocabulary from 1 (most effective) to 5 (least effective). Compare your answers.

_____ Write the words.

_____ Read the words silently.

_____ Say the words aloud.

_____ Use the words in original sentences.

_____ Make a story using the words.

Vocabulary Preview

A The boldfaced words below are from a lecture about memory. Read the sentences below and the definitions on page 18. Match each sentence with the correct definition of the boldfaced word.

_____ **1.** The ***duration*** of a memory can vary. We keep some memories for only a short time and others for our whole lives.

_____ **2.** In order to learn new words, it is ***essential*** to see or hear them several times.

_____ **3.** It's ***conceivable*** that his story is inaccurate; he may have forgotten exactly what happened.

_____ **4.** Infants gain ***visual*** stimulation and input through their eyes. This is a necessary part of learning to judge the speed and distance of objects.

_____ **5.** Scientists have tried to explain ***phenomena*** such as memory.

_____ **6.** Students can remember new vocabulary ***somewhat*** better if they write it down. They won't remember every word, but they will notice an improvement.

_____ **7.** The psychologist's report on memory was very ***detailed***. She used many examples to explain her ideas.

_____ **8.** Our brains store some memories ***temporarily***. Later, we forget them.

_____ **9.** Many of our memories ***fade*** over time, so the details are lost. For example, we may remember having been somewhere but forget the exact date.

_____ **10.** Many people can ***calculate*** simple mathematical problems in their heads.

_____ **11.** Sometimes our memories are ***distorted***. Therefore, we may remember some events inaccurately.

_____ **12.** Scientists have ***distinguished*** three different memory systems.

a. related to sight
b. using a lot of information or facts
c. things that are difficult to understand
d. happening for a limited time
e. a little or slightly
f. able to be believed or imagined
g. gradually become weaker or disappear
h. recognize the difference between two or more similar things
i. measure or compute using numbers
j. important and necessary
k. the length of time that something continues
l. changed from the original or correct meaning

B **The words below are also from the lecture. Read their definitions and the example phrases or sentences.**

impression /ɪm'prɛʃən/ *n* the opinion or feeling you have about someone or something because of the way that he, she, or it seems: *What were your first **impressions of** New York? | **I get the impression that** something's wrong here. | It's important to **make a** good **impression** at your interview.*

long-term /ˌlɔŋ'tɚm/ *adj* continuing for a long period of time into the future: *The long-term effects of the drug are not known.*

memorize /'mɛməˌraɪz/ *v* to learn and remember words, music, or other information: *You all should have your lines memorized by Friday.*

recall /rɪ'kɔl, 'rɪkɔl/ *n* the ability to remember something you have learned or experienced: *She has **total recall*** (ability to remember everything) *of what she has read.*

recognition /ˌrɛkəg'nɪʃən/ *n* knowing who someone is or what something is, because you have seen, heard, experienced, or learned about it in the past

short-term /ˌʃɔrt'tɚm/ *adj* continuing for only a short time into the future: *short-term loans*

C **Use a dictionary to check the pronunciation of the new words in Parts A and B.**

Taking Better Notes

Listing and Numbering Items

When you take notes, grouping related items together will help you understand and remember them. One way to group related items is to list them. You can also number the items in the list.

For example, in a lecture on memory, the speaker discussed three techniques for improving memory. One student listed and numbered the techniques as follows.

IMPROVING MEMORY

1. Use written information—memos, calendars, schedules
2. Use imagery—associate the information with mental images
3. Concentrate—think carefully about information you want to remember

Make a list of five things you have to do this week (for example, do homework, buy groceries). Number the items in the list. Then work with a partner. Student A, tell Student B what you have to do this week. Student B, take notes. Compare the list with the notes. Then change roles.

When you listen to a lecture, try to list and number related items.

Listening to the Lecture

Before You Listen

You will hear a lecture about memory. Write two topics you think the speaker might discuss.

1. ____

2. ____

Listening for Main Ideas

A Close your book. Listen to the lecture and take notes.

B **Use your notes to complete the outline below.**

I. Three types of memory

A. ______________________________

B. ______________________________

C. ______________________________

II. Three ways of measuring memory

A. ______________________________

B. ______________________________

C. ______________________________

Listening for Details

A **Close your book. Listen to the lecture again. Add supporting details to your notes and correct any mistakes.**

B **Use your notes to complete the statements below. Circle the correct answers.**

1. Working memory is also called sensory / short-term / long-term memory.
2. Sensory memory lasts under a half second / more than one second / more than several minutes.
3. Sensory / working / long-term memory allows us to remember things as long as we think about them.
4. Working memory is necessary for doing mathematics / exercising / understanding visual information.
5. We generally remember the main ideas / details / sensory responses of childhood events.
6. Many scientists believe that information stored for longer than one minute / one day / five years is in our long-term memory.
7. The recognition / recall / memorization test involves writing words that you remember seeing.
8. The recognition / recall / memorization test involves looking at a list of words and remembering which words you saw before.
9. The recall / relearning / memorization test involves memorizing a list of words and reviewing it a week later.

Using Your Notes

A **Work with a partner. Exchange notes. Try to find the lists below in your partner's notes:**

1. Three types of memory
2. Three ways of measuring memory

Discuss how to improve the use of lists in your notes.

B **Look at the Note-Taking Tips below. Did you use any of them when you took notes? How can you improve your notes the next time you listen to a lecture?**

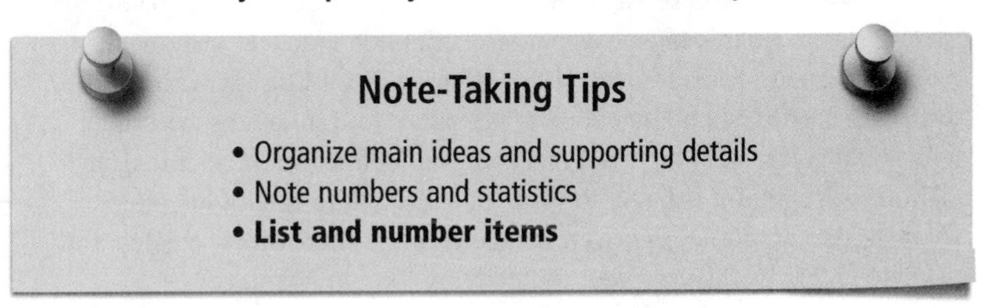

C **Work in small groups. As a group, use your notes to orally reconstruct the lecture, or describe it in detail.**

D **Rewrite or revise your notes so that the organization is clear. If you need to, listen to the lecture again.**

Projects

1. Present a technique you use to remember people's names, vocabulary, or other information. List the steps in the technique. Explain them to your classmates and have them take notes.
2. Read the article. Then answer the questions that follow.

Three Rules for Efficient Learning

A German philosopher, Herman Ebbinghaus, began the scientific study of memory around 120 years ago. Ebbinghaus concentrated on studying how quickly the human mind can remember information. One result of his research is known as the total time hypothesis. This means that the amount you learn depends on the time you spend trying to learn it. In other words, the first rule of efficient learning is that if you study something longer, you tend to learn it more thoroughly.

While it is usually true that studying for four hours is better than studying for one hour, the question remains as to how we should use the four hours. For example, is it better to study for four hours continuously or to study for one hour a day on four consecutive days? The answer, as you may suspect, is that it is better to spread out the study time. The theory that we can learn more efficiently by dividing our practice time is known as the distribution of practice effect. Thus, the second rule of efficient learning is that it is better to study briefly but often.

What is the best way to learn over short periods of time? The answer lies in what is known as micro-distribution practice. Imagine that you are trying to learn some new and rather difficult English vocabulary using flashcards. Should you look at the same word in rapid succession? Or should you look at the word and then wait before you look at it again? The answer is that it is better to wait. This is the third rule of learning.

Two psychologists, Tom Landauer and Robert Bjork, created a technique that works very well for studying foreign language vocabulary. Essentially, you should test a new item after a short delay. Then, as the item becomes better learned, extend the delay. The idea is to test the item after the longest possible interval and yet get it right. Imagine that you have a stack of eight vocabulary cards that you wish to study. You look at the first one on the top of the stack. Because you have not studied it before, you might place it only two cards deep. Because you will see the card again soon, you will probably remember the word. Next, you should extend the delay by placing the card deeper in the stack. If you remember it the next time, you might then place the card at the bottom of the stack.

One advantage of these three rules is that you will learn more efficiently. Another is that you will feel more confident about your ability to learn. Try these techniques before your next vocabulary test. You may find that they work better than your present system!

a. What are the three rules for efficient learning?
b. What specific techniques are suggested?
c. Have you ever tried any of the suggested techniques? If so, describe the results.

3. Find an article in the library or on the Internet about how to improve your memory. Read the article. Take notes on the main ideas and write a one-paragraph summary.

UNIT 4

Psychology

Actions Speak Louder than Words

Topic Preview

Work in small groups. Discuss the questions below.

1. Look at the people in the picture on the left. Describe their expressions and gestures. How do you think they feel?

2. Look at the people in the picture on the right. Describe their expressions and gestures. How do you think they feel?

3. Read the statements. Do you agree or disagree? Write A (agree) or D (disagree).

_____ **a.** There are important differences between verbal[1] and nonverbal[2] communication.

_____ **b.** Nonverbal communication differs from culture to culture.

_____ **c.** You can tell if people are dishonest by watching their nonverbal communication.

_____ **d.** Verbal communication is easier to understand than nonverbal communication.

[1] relating to words or using words

[2] without words

Vocabulary Preview

A The boldfaced words below are from a lecture about non-verbal communication. Read each sentence. Guess the meaning of the boldfaced word.

1. Stefano felt it was an ***invasion*** of his privacy when his mother read his personal letters.
2. We ***convey*** meaning with both verbal and nonverbal communication.
3. Although some of the ideas in the lecture on body language[1] weren't important, the ***bulk*** of them were very useful.
4. Our verbal and nonverbal communication styles are both greatly ***determined*** by how we feel.
5. The Westfield Public Speaking Group is a ***dynamic*** organization. Something new is happening almost every month.
6. It is generally easy to ***differentiate*** between a shy person and an outgoing person. Their body language is rarely similar.
7. The interviewer couldn't understand the politician's answer, so she asked him for ***clarification***.
8. The speaker talked with great ***intensity***; everyone could see how strongly he felt.
9. Nonverbal communication is an ***integral*** part of human communication. Any discussion of how we communicate is incomplete without it.
10. Our understanding of nonverbal communication is ***minimal***. We have a much greater understanding of verbal communication.
11. It was clear from his frown that Mitchell had a negative ***attitude*** toward Sylvie's business proposal.
12. Scientists don't know exactly how much communication is verbal and how much is nonverbal; they can only ***estimate***.

[1] changes in your body position and movements that show what you are feeling and thinking

B **The words below are also from the lecture. Read their definitions and the example phrases or sentences.**

expression /ɪk'sprɛʃən/ *n* a look on someone's face that shows what s/he is thinking or feeling: *a cheerful expression*

gesture /'dʒɛstʃɚ, 'dʒɛʃtʃɚ/ *n* a movement of your arms, hands, or head that shows how you feel about someone or something

intimate /'ɪntəmɪt/ *adj* having a very close relationship with someone: *She told only a few intimate friends that she was pregnant.*

kinesics /kə'nisɪks/ *n* the study of body movements, expressions of the face, etc. as forms of communication

posture /'pɑstʃɚ/ *n* the position you hold your body in when you sit or stand: *Poor posture can lead to back trouble.*

tone /toʊn/ *n* the way your voice sounds that shows how you are feeling or what you mean: *I don't like your* ***tone of voice*** (rude or angry way of speaking). | *He spoke in a threatening tone.*

C **Use a dictionary to check the pronunciation of the new words in Parts A and B.**

Taking Better Notes

Using Abbreviations and Symbols

Using abbreviations and symbols when taking notes can help you to write efficiently and keep up with the speaker. You can use the common abbreviations and symbols below or create your own. However, be very careful that you don't abbreviate too many words or abbreviate them too much. You will often use your notes several weeks after you originally took them. This means that all of your abbreviations and symbols must be clear and easy to understand.

Some common abbreviations and symbols are below.

e.g.	for example	=	equals
i.e.	that is; in other words	≠	does not equal
etc.	et cetera; and so on	vs.	versus; in contrast to
+	and	>	is more than
↑	to rise; to increase	<	is less than
↓	to go down; to decrease	%	percent
→	leads to; causes	$	dollars
←	is caused by; depends on		

You can also use the first syllable or initials of long words and names. For example:

kin = kinesics
nvc = nonverbal communication
fb = feedback
R.B. = Raymond Birdwhistle
com = communication

Do you use any other abbreviations or symbols when you take notes? If so, share them with your classmates.

When you listen to a lecture, try to use abbreviations and symbols in your notes.

Listening to the Lecture

Before You Listen

You will hear a lecture about nonverbal communication. Check (✓) the topics you think the speaker might discuss.

_____ **1.** Why grammar is important in communication

_____ **2.** The kinds of messages our bodies send

_____ **3.** The physical distance we keep between ourselves and other people

_____ **4.** Why only humans use nonverbal communication

_____ **5.** The connection between body language and social status

Listening for Main Ideas

A **Close your book. Listen to the lecture and take notes.**

B **Use your notes to complete the lecture outline below. Use abbreviations and symbols where possible.**

I. Birdwhistle – non-verbal communications (nvc)

A. studied – ____________________

B. believed – ____________________

II. Porter—4 types nvc

A. Physical=_______________=_______________

1. ______________________

a. Distance

b. ______________________

c. ______________________

d. ______________________

2. Dynamic

a. ______________________

b. Gestures

c. ______________________

d. ______________________

B. ______________________

C. Signs

D. ______________________

III. Verb. com. vs. nvc

A. Emot. same—diff. count.

B. ______________________

C. ______________________

D. ______________________

E. ______________________

Listening for Details

A **Close your book. Listen to the lecture again. Add supporting details to your notes and correct any mistakes.**

B **Use your notes to decide if the statements below are true or false. Write T (true) or F (false). Correct the false statements.**

_____ **1.** People spend three-quarters of their waking hours communicating.

_____ **2.** Ten percent to 30 percent of our communication is nonverbal.

_____ **3.** Raymond Birdwhistle began studying nonverbal communication in the 1960s.

_____ **4.** Signal flags and sirens are examples of symbolic nonverbal communication.

_____ **5.** Distance, posture, and physical contact are static features of nonverbal communication.

_____ **6.** Facial expressions provide 55% of the meaning of a message.

_____ **7.** Facial expressions such as smiles have the same meaning in each situation.

_____ **8.** Scientists understand more about hand movements than any other gestures.

_____ **9.** Leaning forward during an interview suggests you are energetic.

Using Your Notes

A Work in small groups. Look at the notes on the first part of the lecture.

Actions more important than words - 70% to 90%
— nvc-communication through actions
— e.g., fac. exp., eyes, voice, body movem't.
Raymond Birdwhistle
— U.S. anthropst.
— studied nvc—early '50s
— "meaning of nvc depends on CONTEXT"
— e.g., a smile—many meanings
"I like you," etc.
"You said someth'g funny"

Are the abbreviations and symbols clear? Discuss how to improve them.

B **Work with a partner. Exchange notes. Look at your partner's notes. Discuss how to improve the use of abbreviations and symbols.**

C **Look at the Note-Taking Tips below. Did you use any of them when you took notes? Which were most helpful? How can you improve your notes the next time you listen to a lecture?**

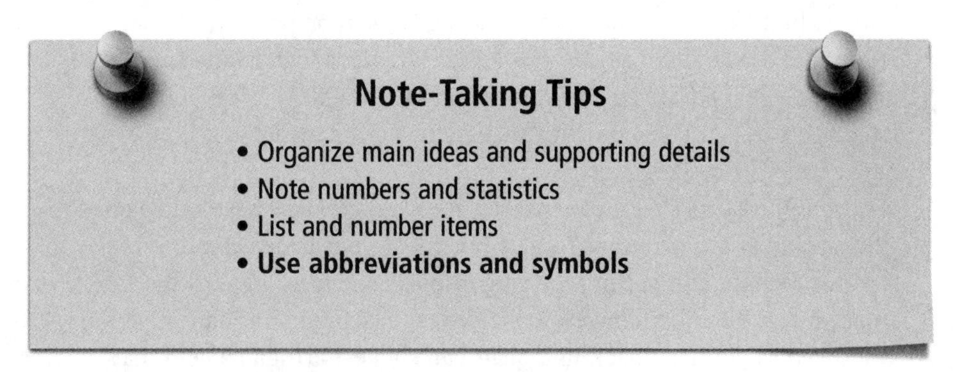

D **Rewrite or revise your notes so that the organization is clear. If you need to, listen to the lecture again. Use your notes to write a summary of the remaining two parts of the lecture.**

Projects

1. Work in small groups. What gesture do you use to express the ideas below? Demonstrate and compare gestures. Which gestures are similar? Which gestures are different?

   Me.
   That person is crazy.
   Stop!
   That's good.
   Come here.
   No.
   I don't know.
   Go away.
   I can't hear you.
   I'm full.

2. Read the excerpt. Then discuss the questions that follow in small groups.

Body Language in Business

In a business context, body language can be particularly important, especially if you are trying to sell a product. Many successful businesses give advice to companies and their employees on body language that is associated with successful salesmanship and how to read clients' body language.

When you first meet a client, for example, it is best to use open gestures. Outward and upward movements of your hands create a positive feeling, and putting the fingertips of one hand against the fingertips of the other conveys confidence. Clasping your hands behind your head as you lean back in a chair can suggest arrogance and may turn away prospective clients. Placing your hands on each side of your waist shows confidence and attracts others. For men, unbuttoning a suit jacket will signify an open attitude, that you're willing to talk or negotiate. Taking off your jacket is really powerful. And rolling up your shirtsleeves suggests you are ready to discuss the final price.

As you talk with prospective clients, watch their body language. If they cross their arms or close their hands, they are probably not receptive to you and your message. You need to relax them and reassure them by sending out body messages that create a positive atmosphere. If you notice them copying your posture and gestures, they are probably interested in your sales presentation. Copying—or "mirroring"—suggests that your clients are receiving and accepting your messages. However, if they cover their mouths, or touch their noses or areas near their eyes, they are withdrawing. In this situation, perhaps you need to try a different approach.

If prospective clients appear defensive or hostile, use only positive signals. Lean slightly forward to put energy into the conversation. Smile from within and without. They'll sense this and be receptive . . . and, quite likely, buy your product!

a. Which parts of the excerpt do you agree with? Why?
b. Which parts of the excerpt do you disagree with? Why?
c. Do you think the information in the excerpt is useful? Why or why not?

3. Spend one day observing how people use gestures. Note the five gestures that are most commonly used. Compare your results as a class.

UNIT 5

Sociology

Marriage: Traditions and Trends

Topic Preview

Work in small groups. Discuss the questions below.

1. Look at the couples in the pictures. Describe their clothing. Where do you think they are from?
2. In your country . . .
   a. what do people wear when they get married?
   b. at what age do people usually get married?
   c. how long do people usually know each other before they get married?
   d. who chooses marriage partners for young people?

Vocabulary Preview

A The boldfaced words below are from a lecture on marriage. Read each sentence. Check (✓) the word that is closest in meaning to the boldfaced word.

1. Over long periods of time, customs can ***erode.*** They are gradually replaced by newer customs.

    _____ **a.** grow stronger

    _____ **b.** grow weaker

    _____ **c.** develop rapidly

2. Although many people ***speculate*** about the future of the family, no one is certain about how it will change.

    _____ **a.** know what will happen

    _____ **b.** argue about what will happen

    _____ **c.** guess what will happen

3. Married couples have different ***obligations*** than single people. For example, they're expected to take care of each other and their children.

    _____ **a.** duties

    _____ **b.** complaints

    _____ **c.** goals

4. Nowadays most people who get married are ***mature.*** It is illegal for children to marry in most countries.

    _____ **a.** very young

    _____ **b.** fully grown

    _____ **c.** completely independent

5. Marrying someone of the same race is the social ***norm*** throughout much of the United States.

    _____ **a.** shocking or exciting situation

    _____ **b.** unusual way of doing something

    _____ **c.** usual way of doing something

6. Children's wishes are often ***subordinate*** to those of their parents. Therefore, they have to do whatever their parents want.

    _____ **a.** less important

    _____ **b.** more important

    _____ **c.** the same

7. Many laws ***preserve*** cultural values. This is one reason why it is difficult to change laws.

_____ **a.** keep

_____ **b.** weaken

_____ **c.** explain

8. New customs, standards, and technology are being introduced in almost every society. As a result, these societies are ***undergoing*** rapid change.

_____ **a.** fighting

_____ **b.** searching for

_____ **c.** experiencing

9. We generally ***conform*** to the behavior of our social group. Behaving differently can create discomfort.

_____ **a.** act happy about

_____ **b.** act angry about

_____ **c.** act like most people

10. Parents sometimes ***restrict*** the amount of time their children spend watching TV. They may allow them to watch only one hour a day.

_____ **a.** limit

_____ **b.** ignore

_____ **c.** forget

11. Marriage is a ***universal*** custom. Every culture has some form of marriage.

_____ **a.** related to the stars and planets

_____ **b.** related to the entire world

_____ **c.** related to one culture

12. Western ***civilization*** today is based on ideas from ancient Greece and Rome.

_____ **a.** well-developed society

_____ **b.** very new society

_____ **c.** society that has disappeared

B **The words below are also from the lecture. Read their definitions and the example phrases or sentences.**

arranged marriage /ə,reɪndʒd 'mærɪdʒ/ *n* a marriage in which the parents choose a husband or wife for their child

extended family /ɪk,stɛndɪd 'fæmli, -məli/ *n* a family that includes parents, children, grandparents, aunts, etc. –compare NUCLEAR FAMILY

nuclear family /,nukliə˞ 'fæmli, -məli/ *n* a family that has a father, mother, and children–compare EXTENDED FAMILY

sanction /'sæŋkʃən/ *v* FORMAL to officially accept or allow something: *Gambling will not be sanctioned in any form.*

socioeconomic /,sousiou,ɛkə'nɑmɪk, ,ikə-/ *adj* relating to both social and economic conditions: *people with a low socioeconomic status*

tribe /traɪb/ *n* a social group that consists of people of the same race who have the same beliefs, customs, language, etc. and live in one area ruled by a chief: *the tribes of the Amazon jungle*

C **Use a dictionary to check the pronunciation of the new words in Parts A and B.**

Taking Better Notes

Making Charts

After listening to a lecture, sometimes making a chart can help you to organize information. A chart can help you understand, summarize, and compare ideas.

For example, the chart below summarizes part of a lecture about traditional and modern Chinese weddings.

	Traditional	**Modern**
Bride's Clothing	red dress	white dress
Groom's Clothing	traditional clothing	suit
Location	home	church or home
Transportation	groom picks up bride on horse or in sedan	groom picks up bride in car
Banquet	groom's family hosts on wedding day; bride's family hosts next day	families of bride and groom host on wedding day only

Work with a partner. Discuss the information in the chart on page 34. Note the similarities and differences between traditional and modern Chinese weddings.

In the following lecture, you will hear about both arranged marriages and love-based marriages. After you listen, you will use your notes to complete a chart.

Listening to the Lecture

Before You Listen

You will hear a lecture about marriage. Write two questions you think the speaker might answer.

1. ____

2. ____

Listening for Main Ideas

A **Close your book. Listen to the lecture and take notes.**

B **Use your notes to complete the sentences below. Circle a, b, or c.**

1. According to the speaker, marriage is a sanctioned union between ________.
   - a. one man and one woman
   - b. one man and one or more women
   - c. one or more men and one or more women

2. According to the speaker, an important part of marriage is that ________.
   - a. obligations are specified
   - b. adoption is allowed
   - c. it is not durable

3. An example of endogamy is marrying someone ________.
   - a. of the same religion
   - b. who speaks a different native language
   - c. with similar ideas about parenthood

4. An example of ________ is not marrying your brother or sister.
   - a. exogamy
   - b. endogamy
   - c. gender bias

5. Greater exogamy might result in ________.
   a. smaller families
   b. more interracial marriages
   c. higher divorce rates
6. Arranged marriages are characteristic of societies in which ________ are common.
   a. extended families
   b. nuclear families
   c. child marriages

Listening for Details

A **Close your book. Listen to the lecture again. Add supporting details to your notes and correct any mistakes.**

B **Use your notes to correct the mistakes in the statements below. Compare your answers in small groups.**

1. The institution of marriage is several million years old.
2. The institution of marriage is disappearing.
3. Adoption is an example of gender bias.
4. Endogamy is not important in most societies.
5. The speaker has a brother whose marriage is an example of endogamy.
6. Traditionally, marriage was a private decision between two people.
7. Marrying for love was common in ancient societies.
8. Extended families are replacing nuclear families in many countries.

Using Your Notes

A **Work with a partner. Use your notes to complete the chart about arranged marriages and love marriages. Compare your charts as a class.**

	Arranged Marriages	Love Marriages
When Common	from ancient times	relatively recent
Who Chooses Partner		
Dating		
Romance		
Type of Family		

B **Look at the Note-Taking Tips below. Did you use any of them when you took notes? Which were most helpful? How can you improve your notes the next time you listen to a lecture?**

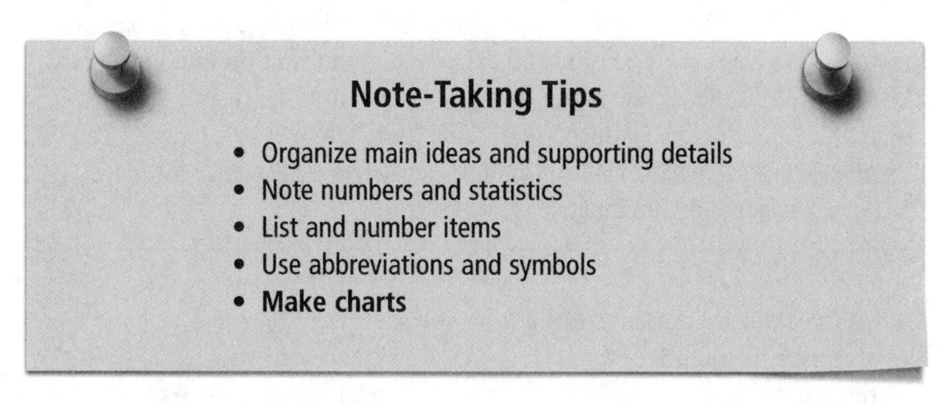

C **Work in small groups. As a group, use your notes to orally reconstruct the lecture, or describe it in detail.**

D **Rewrite or revise your notes so that the organization is clear. If you need to, listen to the lecture again.**

Projects

1. What is important in a marriage partner? Rank the items below from 1 (most important) to 6 (least important). You will need to add one item to the list. Compare your answers in a small group.

   _____ Personality

   _____ Wealth

   _____ Appearance

   _____ Similarity of interests

   _____ Intelligence

   _____ ____________________

2. The letter that follows was written to an advice columnist. Read the letter. Then write a letter in response. Compare your letters in small groups.

> Dear Dora,
>
> I desperately need help with a terrible problem. I was married two years ago at age 20, and the first year was heavenly. Gregory, my husband, was helpful and supportive in every way possible. However, about a year ago, I noticed that he was beginning to change. Whenever he came home, he told me how busy he was at work and how exhausted he was. I was sympathetic, so I told him to relax, watch TV, or take a nap before dinner. After a few months of this, I noticed that he had almost completely stopped doing any work around the house. He was coming home and expecting me to wait on him constantly. I also work full time, so the strain of my job plus all of the responsibilities around the house is exhausting. I really don't know how much longer I can do this. Please tell me what I can do to return to marriage heaven.
>
> Exhausted in Cincinnati

3. Give a five-minute presentation about one aspect of marriage in your country. Possible aspects include:

   dating customs
   typical age of bride and groom
   parental involvement
   special customs or laws
   the marriage ceremony
   special wedding clothing

UNIT 6

Astronomy

Black Holes, White Holes, and Wormholes

Topic Preview

Work in small groups. Discuss the questions below.

1. Look at the picture. How and from where do you think it was taken?
2. Do you think space travel is important? Why or why not?
3. Do you think time travel is possible? Why or why not?

Vocabulary Preview

A The boldfaced words below are from a lecture about astronomy. Read each sentence. Guess the meaning of the boldfaced word.

1. As the rocket moved farther into space, the earth seemed to ***shrink*** in size minute by minute.
2. The rocket's speed was ***constant***, neither increasing nor decreasing.
3. The earth ***rotates*** once every twenty-four hours.
4. Space exploration is a ***controversial*** subject. Some people support it, while others think it is too expensive.
5. Scientists don't usually accept a theory until there is ***empirical*** evidence to prove it.
6. Many people ***deny*** the possibility of time travel; they think it is impossible.
7. Because they were built from the same plans, the two spaceships look ***identical***.
8. Some people believe that it's possible to travel through time ***via*** a time machine.
9. After the explosion, the planet ***ceased*** to exist. It was completely gone.
10. A violent earthquake caused NASA's research building to ***collapse***.
11. Many people don't understand complex scientific ***concepts***. The ideas are too difficult.
12. The new space station is extremely ***stable***. Even a nearby explosion won't harm it.

B The words below are also from the lecture. Read their definitions and the example phrases or sentences.

compress /kəm'prɛs/ *v* to press something or make it smaller so that it takes up less space: *The garlic is dried and* ***compressed into*** *a pill.*

dense /dɛns/ *adj* a substance that is dense has a lot of mass in relation to its size: *Water is eight hundred times denser than air.*

gravitational /ˌgrævə'teɪʃənl/ *adj* TECHNICAL relating to or resulting from the force of gravity: *the earth's gravitational pull*

mass /mæs/ *n* TECHNICAL the amount of material in something: *The sun makes up about 99.9 percent of the mass of the solar system.*

matter /'mæt̬ɚ/ *n* TECHNICAL the material that everything in the universe is made of, including solids, liquids, and gases

particle /'part̬ɪkəl/ *n* one of the very small pieces of matter that an atom consists of: *subatomic particles such as protons*

C Use a dictionary to check the pronunciation of the new words in Parts A and B.

Taking Better Notes

Drawing Sketches

You may have heard the expression, "A picture is worth a thousand words." Sketches can be very powerful because they help you to *visualize* and *remember* ideas. Sometimes it is easier to draw a simple sketch than to write down information, especially if the information is complex. Adding labels to the sketch can help make the sketch clear.

For example, the student sketches below clearly show the positions of the sun, earth, and moon during a lunar eclipse.

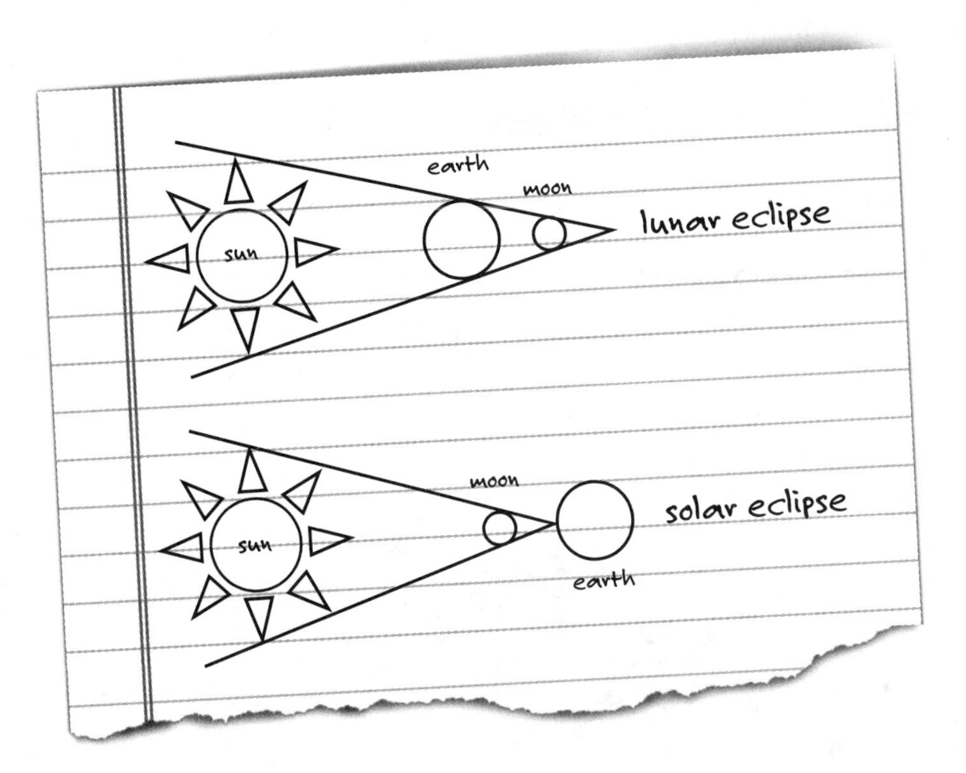

Draw a sketch of a machine or other device that contains several items or parts (for example, a bicycle, photocopier, or CD player). Work with a partner. Student A, use your sketch to describe the machine or device, explaining the position and function of each item or part. Student B, draw and label a sketch based on Student A's description. Compare sketches. Then change roles.

When you listen to a lecture, try to include sketches in your notes.

Listening to the Lecture

Before You Listen

You will hear a lecture about astronomy. Check (✓) the topics you think the speaker might discuss.

_____ **1.** How black holes are created

_____ **2.** Famous astrologers

_____ **3.** Whether time travel is possible

_____ **4.** The connection between black holes and white holes

_____ **5.** The history of space flight

Listening for Main Ideas

A **Close your book. Listen to the lecture and take notes.**

B **Use your notes to label each sketch. Use the words from the list.**

singularity	black hole	gravitational force
white hole	wormhole	event horizon

1.

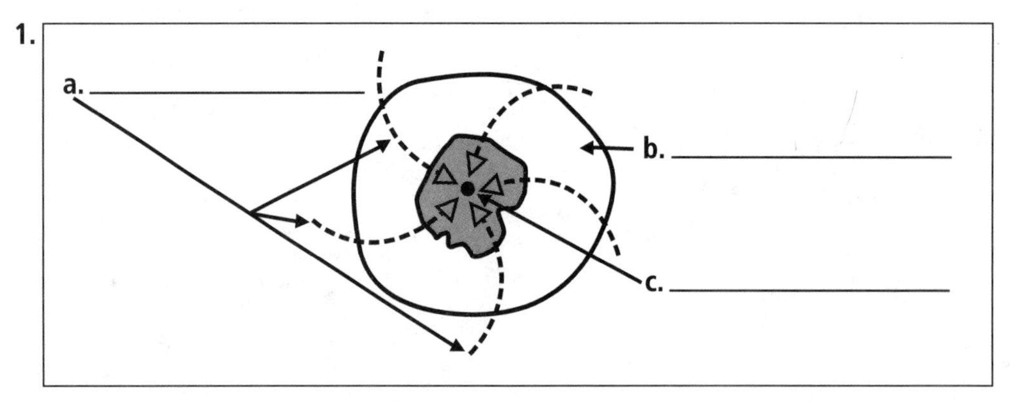

2.

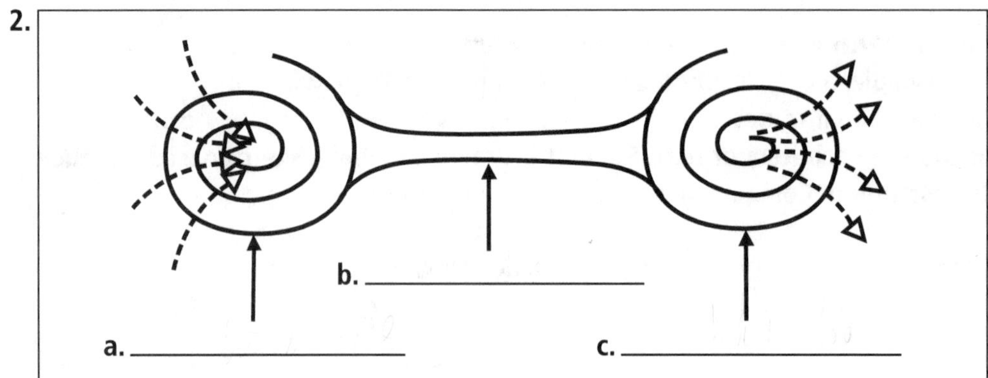

Listening for Details

A **Close your book. Listen to the lecture again. Add supporting details to your notes and correct any mistakes.**

B **Use your notes to decide if the statements below are true or false. Write T (true) or F (false). Correct the false statements. Compare your answers in small groups.**

_____ **1.** The term "black hole" describes the final stage in the life of a small star.

_____ **2.** We can't see black holes because light can't escape from them.

_____ **3.** When a star collapses, its gravitational pull increases.

_____ **4.** The smaller the size of a collapsing star, the greater its gravitational pull.

_____ **5.** The singularity of a black hole is very dense and lightweight.

_____ **6.** Matter pours into a white hole.

_____ **7.** There is no empirical evidence for wormholes.

_____ **8.** In theory, time travel through non-rotating black holes is possible.

_____ **9.** There is mathematical proof that wormholes exist.

_____ **10.** Wormholes are stable.

Using Your Notes

A **Work with a partner. Exchange notes. Take turns using your partner's sketches to explain the concepts in the lecture. Discuss how to make the sketches clearer.**

B **Look at the Note-Taking Tips below. Did you use any of them when you took notes? Which were most helpful? How can you improve your notes the next time you listen to a lecture?**

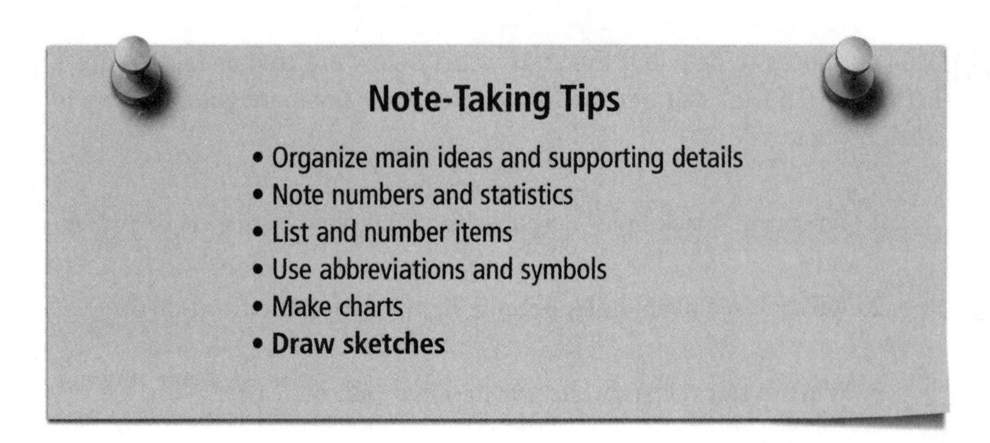

C **Work in small groups. As a group, use your notes to make an oral summary of the lecture.**

D **Rewrite or revise your notes so that the organization is clear. Label any unclear sketches. If you need to, listen to the lecture again.**

Projects

1. Work in small groups. Imagine that you can travel back in time. Decide which historical period you would most like to visit. Discuss your reasons and write them below. Then share your ideas as a class.

Historical Period: ______________________________

Reasons:

a. ______________________________

b. ______________________________

c. ______________________________

d. ______________________________

e. ______________________________

2. As a class, make a questionnaire about time travel. Write at least five questions. (For example: *If time travel were possible, what would the advantages be? If you could change one past event, what would it be?*) Give the questionnaire to at least three people. Summarize their responses. Compare and discuss your answers as a class.

3. Research a topic related to astronomy in the library or on the Internet. Possible topics include:

the expanding universe	quasars	comets
spiral galaxies	supernovae	pulsars

   Give a five-minute presentation of your findings to the class. Use sketches as visual aids in your presentation.

UNIT 7

Cognitive Linguistics

Animal Talk

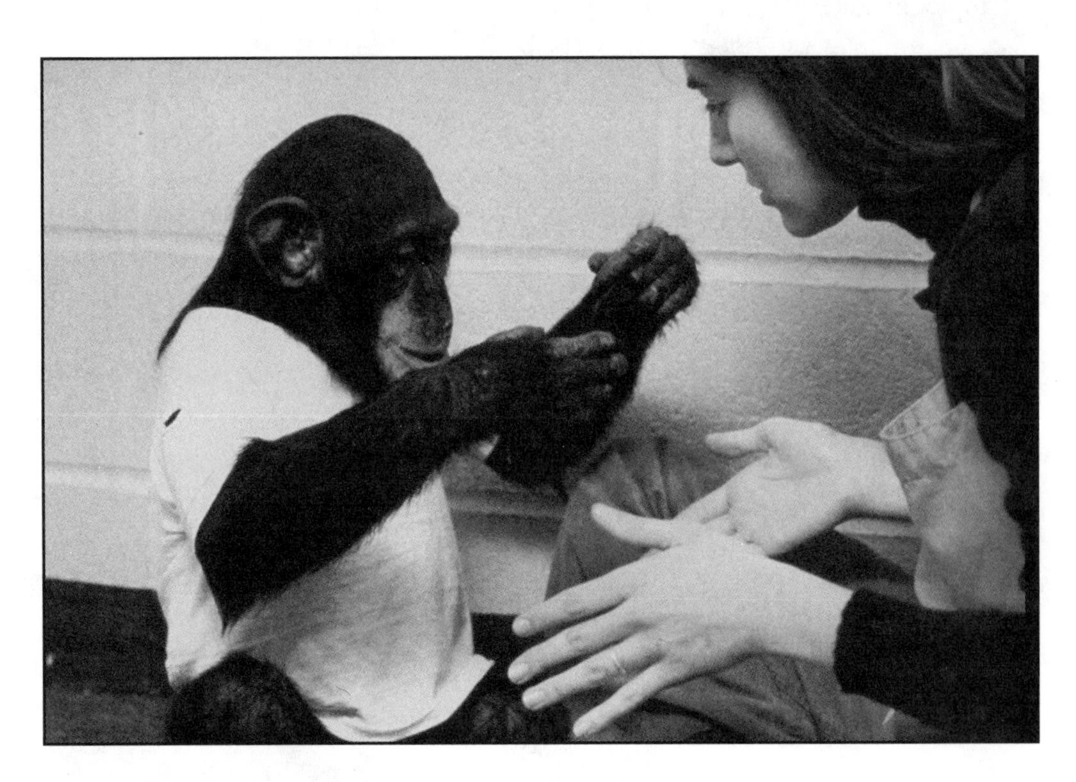

Topic Preview

Work in small groups. Discuss the questions below.

1. What animal is pictured? What do you think it is doing?
2. Have you ever had a pet? If so, how did you communicate with it? How did it communicate with you?
3. Read each statement below. Write T if you think it is true and F if you think it is false. Compare and explain your answers.

_____ **a.** Some animals can use words.

_____ **b.** Some animals can make sentences.

_____ **c.** Some animals can lie.

_____ **d.** All animals communicate with members of their own species.

_____ **e.** Many animals can communicate emotion.

Vocabulary Preview

A The boldfaced words below are from a lecture about animal communication. Read each sentence. Circle the letter of the word or phrase that is closest in meaning to the boldfaced word.

1. Monkeys are generally ***tranquil***, but if an enemy approaches, they become afraid and run away.
   a. excited
   b. interesting
   c. calm

2. Animal communication is not a ***straightforward*** subject. It's complicated because animals communicate differently with each other.
   a. impossible to understand
   b. difficult to understand
   c. easy to understand

3. I couldn't understand what the child said because words were in the wrong ***sequence***.
   a. order
   b. spelling
   c. book

4. The boy was ***deceitful*** when he yelled, "Fire!" Actually, there was no fire.
   a. honest
   b. dishonest
   c. excited

5. Although some animals appear to communicate, scientists cannot ***confirm*** that they actually use language.
   a. conduct research
   b. disagree with
   c. be certain

6. Humans can use language ***deceptively*** by telling lies or half-truths.
   a. in an honest way
   b. in a dishonest way
   c. in a serious way

7. Most animals can communicate with members of their own ***species***, but not with other groups.
   a. specialized researchers
   b. type of animal
   c. geographical area

8. Some animals make ***identical*** sounds when they sense danger. Thus, they appear to be communicating with each other.
   a. loud
   b. different
   c. the same

9. ***Contrary*** to what you might think, not all animal sounds communicate meaning.
   a. in order
   b. similar
   c. opposite

10. Some birds can ***manipulate*** their sounds to make many different songs.
    a. sing loudly
    b. use skillfully
    c. repeat constantly

11. Animals tend to be ***rigid*** in their use of language. They generally don't communicate in different ways.
    a. unchanging
    b. creative
    c. simple

12. Grammar is a human ***innovation***. It's not present in animal communication.
    a. difficult subject
    b. new idea
    c. unsolved problem

B The words below are also from the lecture. Read the definitions and example phrases or sentences.

decode /di'koʊd/ *v* TECHNICAL to understand the meaning of a word rather than use a word to express meaning—opposite ENCODE

encode /ɪn'koʊd/ *v* to put a message or other information into code—opposite DECODE

referent /'rɛfrənt/ *n* the object, person, idea, etc. that a word means

scan /skæn/ *v* to examine an area carefully, because you are looking for a particular person or thing: *Lookouts were* **scanning** *the sky* **for** *enemy planes.*

ultrasonic /ˌʌltrə'sɑnɪk◂/ *adj* TECHNICAL sounds that are too high for humans to hear

vibration /vaɪ'breɪʃən/ *n* a continuous slight shaking movement: *the vibrations of the plane's engines*

C Use a dictionary to check the pronunciation of the new words in Parts A and B.

Taking Better Notes

Noting Descriptions

In a lecture that includes description, it is important to note the main descriptive words and phrases. This will help you remember specific information about how something or someone looks, sounds, or behaves. One way to note descriptions is to write the key features on the left-hand side of the page. Then write the descriptive words or phrases next to the key features.

Look at the lecture excerpt and example student notes below.

> . . . A standing chimpanzee is from 3.75 to 5.5 feet tall. Male chimps weigh from 123 to 176 pounds, and female chimps weigh from 99 to 149 pounds. Chimps are also one of the noisiest animals in the jungle. They like to scream, drum on trees, slap the ground, and make other sounds almost continuously. Even when they are alone, chimps make a lot of noise. In fact, they seem to talk to themselves quite a lot. Chimpanzees use touch when they greet one another. They touch fingertips and even hug one another sometimes . . .

CHIMPS
—Height —3.75–5.5 feet (standing)
—Weight —123–176 pounds (male)
—99–149 pounds (female)
—Sounds —Very noisy—scream, hit things, make sounds all the time
—alone—talk to self
—Touch —Greet by touching fingertips, hugs

Work with a partner. Student A, describe an animal. Include as many descriptive words and phrases as possible. Student B, take notes. Compare the notes with the description. Then change roles.

When you listen to a lecture, try to include descriptive words and phrases in your notes.

Listening to the Lecture

Before You Listen

You will hear a lecture about animal communication. Write two topics you think the speaker might discuss.

1. ______________________________

2. ______________________________

Listening for Main Ideas

A Close your book. Listen to the lecture and take notes.

B Use your notes to answer the questions below. Circle a, b, or c.

1. What is affective communication?
  a. communication of emotion
  b. persuasive communication
  c. communication of information

2. What is symbolic communication?
  a. communication about abstract topics
  b. communication with grammatical accuracy
  c. communication about specific referents

3. Do birds intend to communicate?
  a. We don't know.
  b. Yes, with their own species.
  c. Yes, with many species.

4. Can animals speak in sentences?
  a. No.
  b. Yes, a little.
  c. Yes, but with poor grammar.

5. How is human communication different from animal communication?
  a. Humans use language symbolically.
  b. Humans require an audience.
  c. Humans can manipulate language.

Listening for Details

A **Close your book. Listen to the lecture again. Add supporting details to your notes and correct any mistakes.**

B **Use your notes to answer the questions.**

1. Why is it difficult to study animal communication?

 ____

2. What are some common ways that animals communicate?

 ____

3. What types of alarm calls do vervet monkeys use?

 ____

4. What kinds of animals use food calls?

 ____

5. Do scientists think that chickens consciously lie? Why or why not?

 ____

6. What two factors affect whether birds make food calls?

 ____

7. How are bird songs created?

 ____

8. What are three possible purposes for bird songs?

 ____

Using Your Notes

A **Work with a partner. Exchange notes. Take turns using your partner's notes to describe the following behaviors.**

1. The speaker's dog when the speaker is sad or tired
2. A vervet monkey when it hears a leopard alarm call
3. A vervet monkey when it hears an eagle alarm call
4. A vervet monkey when it hears a snake alarm call
5. A male chicken when known female chickens are present
6. A male chicken when unknown female chickens are present

Discuss how to make the descriptions in your notes clearer.

B **Look at the Note-Taking Tips below. Did you use any of them when you took notes? Which were most helpful? How can you improve your notes the next time you listen to a lecture?**

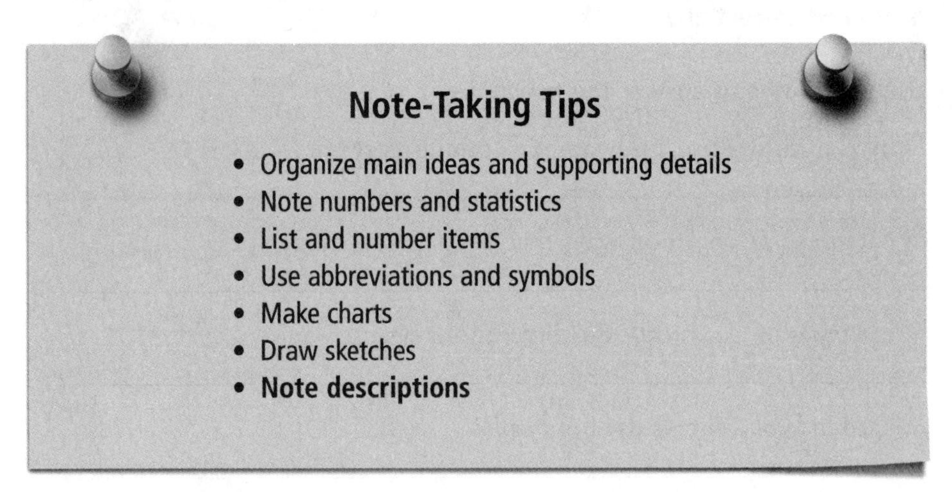

Note-Taking Tips

- Organize main ideas and supporting details
- Note numbers and statistics
- List and number items
- Use abbreviations and symbols
- Make charts
- Draw sketches
- **Note descriptions**

C **Work in small groups. As a group, use your notes to orally reconstruct the lecture, or describe it in detail.**

D **Rewrite or revise your notes so that the organization is clear. If you need to, listen to the lecture again.**

Projects

1. Work in small groups. Make a questionnaire about pets. Write at least five questions. (For example: *What kind of pets have you owned?*) Then interview three people. Compare and discuss their answers as a group. Report your findings to the class.

2. Choose a pet that you have never owned before (for example, a special breed of dog, a ferret, or a hamster). Conduct library or Internet research about the pet. Prepare a five-minute presentation for your classmates. You may want to include the information below.

   a description of the pet — why you want the pet
   how to care for the pet — a picture of the pet

3. Read an article from the library or the Internet about animal communication. Write a one-paragraph summary of the article. Then write a one-paragraph response, stating your opinion about the article.

Gender Differences in Language

Topic Preview

Work in small groups. Discuss the questions below.

1. Look at the picture. Describe what the children are doing.
2. Who did you play with when you were a child? What games did you play? What did you talk about?
3. Who do you spend your free time with now? What things do you talk about?
4. Do you agree or disagree with the following statements? Write A (agree) or D (disagree). Compare and explain your answers.

_____ Men and women communicate differently.

_____ It's important to understand how men and women communicate differently.

_____ Male and female communication styles are becoming more similar.

_____ Inherited biological factors have more influence on communication style than social environment.

_____ Men use nonverbal communication more skillfully than women.

Vocabulary Preview

A The boldfaced words below are from a lecture about male and female communication. Read each sentence. Guess the meaning of the boldfaced word. Compare your answers in small groups.

1. People often have the ***stereotype*** that women are kinder, more considerate, and less aggressive than men. This is not always true, of course!
2. Different speaking styles among different social groups can result in ***segregation***. Communities that speak one way might not mix with communities that speak differently.
3. ***Contemporary*** language includes many slang expressions that used to be considered unacceptable.
4. The style of the magazine article gave me the ***impression*** that the author was male.
5. If a marriage is to be successful, it's ***crucial*** that both partners understand each other's "language."
6. Our deeply held ideas about male and female communication are often ***reinforced*** by the movies we watch and the books we read.
7. Nowadays, men and women ***exhibit*** increasingly similar communication styles.
8. We normally ***establish*** our patterns of language behavior early in life.
9. It's not clear exactly how much of one's communication style is ***inherent*** and how much is learned after birth.
10. The way people talk can have a ***dramatic*** effect on their career opportunities.
11. Much research has been ***devoted to*** understanding the causes of gender differences in language.
12. Men and women typically ***engage in*** different kinds of conversations.

B **The words below are also from the lecture. Read their definitions and the example phrases or sentences.**

collaboration /kəˌlæbəˈreɪʃən/ *n* the act of working together to make or produce something: *Our departments worked* ***in close collaboration*** *on the project.*

condition /kənˈdɪʃən/ *v* to make a person or animal think or behave in a particular way by influencing or training them over a period of time: **[condition sb to (do) sth]** *The American public has been conditioned to think that this is just the way things are.*

genetic /dʒəˈnɛt̬ɪk/ *adj* relating to GENES or GENETICS: *They now have a genetic test for that disease.* | *genetic mutations*

nature /ˈneɪtʃɚ/ *n* everything that exists in the world that is not made or controlled by humans, such as animals, plants, weather, etc.: *We like camping; it makes us feel closer to nature.*

nurture /ˈnɚtʃɚ/ *n* FORMAL the education and care that you are given as a child, and the way it affects your later development and attitudes

-oriented /ɔriɛnɪd/ [in adjectives] **work-oriented/family-oriented, etc.** mainly concerned with or paying attention to work, family, etc.: *an export-oriented company* | *The resort offers a variety of family-oriented entertainment.*

C **Use a dictionary to check the pronunciation of the new words in Parts A and B.**

Taking Better Notes

Noting Comparisons and Contrasts

In a lecture that includes comparisons and contrasts, it is important to note how items are similar or different.

The words and phrases below are used to indicate similarities, or comparisons.

like	likewise	as . . . as
also	ditto	as with . . . so too with . . .
not only . . . but also	similar to / similarly	in a similar manner
both . . . and . . .	parallels	in like fashion
in the same way		

The words and phrases below are used to indicate differences, or contrasts.

but	more (than)	whereas
while	less (than)	on the other hand
different from	rather than	dissimilar to
in contrast	unlike	although
however	conversely	

One way to take notes that compare and contrast two or more items is to note each item separately, and then note the similarities and differences. Look at the example below.

FORMAL COMMUNICATION
— no slang
— complete sentences
— polite forms
INFORMAL COMMUNICATION
— some slang
— incomplete sentences
— fewer polite forms

Another way is to note each point of comparison and contrast separately. Look at the example below.

	FORMAL	INFORMAL
Vocabulary:	no slang	some slang
Sentences:	complete	incomplete
Forms:	polite	fewer polite

Work with a partner. Student A, compare and contrast people you know well (for example, two family members). Explain the similarities and differences. Student B, take notes. Compare the notes with the explanation. Then change roles.

When you listen to a lecture, try to include some comparisons and contrasts in your notes.

Listening to the Lecture

Before You Listen

You will hear a lecture about male and female communication styles. Check (✓) the topics you think the speaker might discuss.

_____ **1.** Why men and women speak different languages

_____ **2.** How schools affect communication styles

_____ **3.** How boys' and girls' playtime activities differ

_____ **4.** How men's and women's clothing styles differ

_____ **5.** How social status affects communication styles

_____ **6.** How genetics affects communication style

_____ **7.** Male and female socialization patterns

Listening for Main Ideas

A **Close your book. Listen to the lecture and take notes.**

B **Use your notes to answer the questions below. Two answers are correct. Cross out the incorrect answer.**

1. Why is communication style important?
- **a.** It affects how people see and respond to us.
- **b.** It shows how we see our own status.
- **c.** It teaches us about the structure of the brain.

2. According to the speaker, what are the main causes of language differences?
- **a.** genetic factors
- **b.** contemporary books
- **c.** socialization

3. In general, how do male and female communication styles differ?
   a. Male communication is more competition-oriented.
   b. Female communication is more family-oriented.
   c. Women use nonverbal communication more skillfully.

4. How do parental communication styles differ?
   a. Mothers are more controlling than fathers.
   b. Fathers are more supportive than mothers.
   c. Fathers are more concerned with identifying problems than mothers.

5. According to the speaker, what are the main purposes of men's communication?
   a. to achieve goals
   b. to establish relationships
   c. to give information

6. According to the speaker, what might cause male and female communication styles to become more similar?
   a. changing children's playtime activities
   b. decreasing segregation between boys and girls
   c. increasing women's authority in the workplace

Listening for Details

A **Close your book. Listen to the lecture again. Add supporting details to your notes and correct any mistakes.**

B **Use your notes to decide if the statements below are true or false. Write T (true) or F (false). Correct the false statements.**

_____ 1. Most students are interested in the issue of gender differences in communication.

_____ 2. We spend 60 percent of our working hours communicating.

_____ 3. Genetic factors do not influence male and female communication styles.

_____ 4. Playing house can help create a collaboration-oriented communication style.

_____ 5. Having discussions about relationships helps develop a competition-oriented communication style.

_____ **6.** Traditional gender roles affect how parents talk to their children.

_____ **7.** Between the 1920s and the 1990s, women's conversations about work and money rose over 30 percent.

_____ **8.** Male and female communication styles are the same in all cultures.

Using Your Notes

A **Work with a partner. Exchange notes. Take turns using your partner's notes to compare and contrast the following items.**

1. Boys' and girls' activities
2. Fathers' and mothers' communication with children
3. Purposes of men's and women's communication
4. Men's and women's topics of communication
5. Men's and women's body language

Discuss how to make the comparisons and contrasts in your notes clearer.

B **Look at the Note-Taking Tips below. Did you use any of them when you took notes? Which were most helpful? How can you improve your notes the next time you listen to a lecture?**

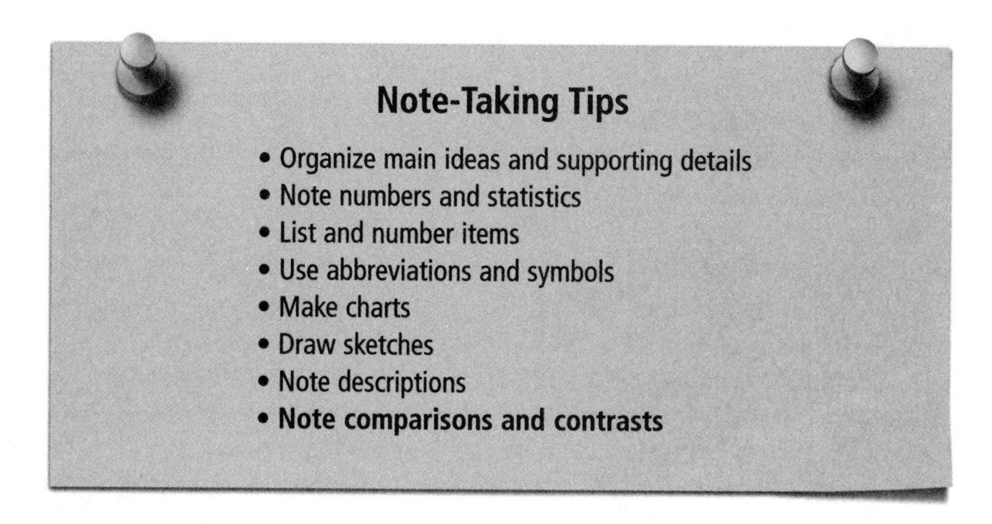

C **Rewrite or revise your notes so that the organization is clear. If you need to, listen to the lecture again.**

D **Use your notes to write a summary of the lecture.**

Projects

1. In small groups, review your lecture notes. List the speaker's conclusions. Then discuss the questions below.
   a. In your opinion, which of the speaker's conclusions are generally true? Why?
   b. In your opinion, which of the speaker's conclusions are stereotypes? Why?
   c. What other factors might influence gender differences in communication?

2. Work with a partner. Compare and contrast how men and women communicate in your culture. Make a chart showing the similarities and differences. Compare your charts as a class.

3. Record a three- to five-minute English conversation from a television show or video. Then transcribe it. Bring your transcription to class and read it aloud. Have your classmates guess whether the speakers are men or women. Ask them what factors influenced their decision.

Fashion Design

Fashion and Status

Topic Preview

Work in small groups. Discuss the questions below.

1. Look at the people in the picture. What can you say about their characters and lifestyles? Write five words to describe each person.
2. Can you judge people by the clothes they wear? If so, how? If not, why not?
3. Do you think that fashion and status are connected? If so, how?

Vocabulary Preview

A The boldfaced words below are from a lecture about fashion and status. Read the sentences and the definitions that follow. Match each sentence with the correct definition of the boldfaced word.

_____ 1. Sylvie ***abandoned*** her plan to buy an expensive evening gown because she didn't have enough money.

_____ 2. Many people think wearing expensive jewelry gives them ***prestige***.

_____ 3. Linda never wears more than two colors ***simultaneously***. Today she's dressed in black and red.

_____ 4. Examples of tenth-century clothing are very ***scarce***. Only a few can be found in the best museums.

_____ 5. Richard wore his new vest for three days ***consecutively***. On the fourth day, he finally wore something different.

_____ 6. In ***hierarchical*** societies, the wealthy tend to wear more expensive clothes than the middle and lower classes.

_____ 7. Clothes made from ***inferior*** materials usually don't last very long.

_____ 8. Her pink jacket and orange hair made her very ***conspicuous*** in the crowd.

_____ 9. Clothing styles are frequently used as ***vehicles*** for expressing one's personality.

_____10. Conservative rather than ***radical*** clothes are the best choice for job interviews.

_____11. In most private schools, students must ***conform*** to a strict dress code.

_____12. Young people often have very ***definite*** ideas about what clothes are fashionable.

a. at the same time
b. stopped doing or using
c. easy to notice
d. having different ranks or levels
e. one after another
f. clear and certain
g. means of doing or showing
h. status or respect
i. lower-quality
j. extreme or very different
k. rare or uncommon
l. follow an established pattern

B **The words below are also from the lecture. Read their definitions and the example phrases or sentences.**

artificial /ˌɑrt̬əˈfɪʃəl◂/ *adj* not natural, but made by people: *artificial sweeteners | an artificial leg*

brand name /ˈbrænd ˌneɪm/ *n* the name a company gives to the goods it has produced: *brand names such as Jell-O® and Coca-Cola®*

conspicuous consumption /kənˌspɪkjuəs kənˈsʌmpʃən/ *n* wasteful spending intended to attract attention and show one's wealth and high social position, especially done by people who have recently become wealthy and want other people to know it

garment /ˈgɑrmənt/ *n* FORMAL a piece of clothing

off-the-rack /ˌɔf ðə ˈræk/ *adj* off-the-rack clothes are not made to fit one particular person, but are made in standard sizes

trademark /ˈtreɪdmɑrk/ *n* a special name, mark, or word on a product that shows it is made by a particular company

C **Use a dictionary to check the pronunciation of the new words in Parts A and B.**

Taking Better Notes

Noting Definitions

When giving lectures, speakers may use key words that have special or limited meanings. They sometimes give brief definitions of these key words to help you better understand the lecture.

Sometimes key words are followed by their definitions. The phrases below are used to introduce definitions.

X is/are . . .
X focuses on . . .
X means . . .
. . . X, which is . . .
. . . X, where . . .

Sometimes definitions precede the key words. In this case, the phrases below may be used.

. . . called X, . . .
. . . We call this X.
. . . referred to as X, . . .
. . . This is (what's) known as X.

When noting definitions, it may be helpful to write the key word or expression in large letters on the left-hand side of the page and write the definition beside or underneath it. Look at the examples below.

Find definitions for two words related to fashion or clothing (for example, a garment or fabric) and write them down. Then work with a partner. Student A, explain the meanings of the two words. Student B, take notes. Compare the notes with the explanation. Then change roles.

When you listen to a lecture, try to include some definitions in your notes.

Listening to the Lecture

Before You Listen

You will hear a lecture about fashion and status. Cross out the three topics you think the speaker is least likely to mention.

1. Where people buy their clothes
2. Why people buy the clothes they do
3. How people show their wealth through the things they buy
4. How to dress better for work
5. The history of Gucci
6. What makes clothes high status

Listening for Main Ideas

A Close your book. Listen to the lecture and take notes.

B Use your notes to complete the outline below.

I. Sumptuary Laws

Definition:______________________________

II. Conspicuous Consumption—8 types

A. ______________________________

Definition:______________________________

B. ______________________________

Definition:______________________________

C. ______________________________

Definition:______________________________

D. ______________________________

Definition:______________________________

E. ______________________________

Definition:______________________________

F. ______________________________

Definition:______________________________

G. ______________________________

Definition:______________________________

H. ______________________________

Definition:______________________________

Listening for Details

A Close your book. Listen to the lecture again. Add supporting details to your notes and correct any mistakes.

B **Use your notes to answer the questions below.**

1. Why did sumptuary laws become difficult to enforce?

___

___

2. Give an example of conspicuous addition at the beach.

___

___

3. Give an example of conspicuous multiplication among very wealthy men.

___

___

4. What materials were prestigious in the past? Why?

___

___

5. What materials are prestigious today? Why?

___

___

6. Why are clothes with designer labels expensive?

___

___

7. Why do some designer garments have labels on the outside?

___

___

8. Give an example of conspicuous outrage.

___

___

Using Your Notes

A **Work with a partner. Exchange notes. Take turns using your partner's notes to define the following expressions.**

1. Associative consumption
2. Conspicuous addition
3. Conspicuous consumption
4. Conspicuous division
5. Conspicuous labeling
6. Conspicuous materials
7. Conspicuous multiplication
8. Conspicuous outrage
9. Conspicuous wealth
10. Sumptuary laws

Discuss how to make the definitions in your notes clearer.

B **Check your notes against the Note-Taking Tips below. Did you use any of the tips when you took notes? Which were most helpful? How can you improve your notes the next time you listen to a lecture?**

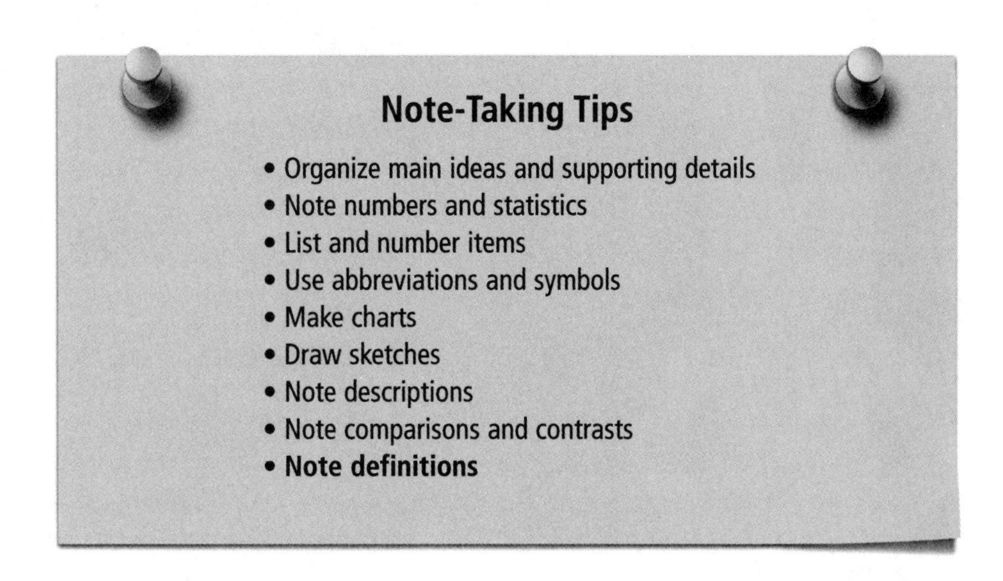

C **In small groups, use your notes to orally reconstruct the lecture, or explain it in detail.**

D **Rewrite or revise your notes so that the organization is clear. If you need to, listen to the lecture again.**

Projects

1. How do people in your culture traditionally use clothes to indicate social status? Has this changed in recent years? If so, how? Give a five-minute presentation about this topic to the class.
2. Find two pictures of clothing styles—one that you think indicates high status and one that you think indicates low status. Bring them to class. In a small group, explain your choices and the reasons for them.
3. Read an article from the library or the Internet about one of the topics below.

   sumptuary laws
   conspicuous consumption
   current fashions
   a famous designer
   a type of fabric
   fashion marketing techniques

   Write a one-paragraph summary of the article.

UNIT 10

Behavioral Science

The Making of Genius

Pablo Picasso

Michael Jordan

Wolfgang Amadeus Mozart

Topic Preview

Work in small groups. Discuss the questions below.

1. Look at the pictures. Why is each person famous?
2. Have you ever met a skilled artist, athlete, or musician? How do you think he or she became so skilled?
3. Do you think people are born with natural talent? Or do you think they become skilled by practicing for a long time?

Vocabulary Preview

A The boldfaced words below are from a lecture about the making of genius. Read each sentence. Circle the letter of the word or phrase that is closest in meaning to the boldfaced word.

1. Tania said she couldn't have won the music award without the ***support*** of her parents and teachers.
   a. help
   b. success
   c. failure

2. Some personality characteristics are ***innate***; others are learned after birth.
   a. studied
   b. natural
   c. false

3. Some parents believe they can ***detect*** talent in their children. They tell their friends that their one-year-old is a genius.
   a. ignore
   b. encourage
   c. notice

4. He only has average general ***intelligence***, but he is an excellent artist.
   a. ability to think
   b. ability to succeed
   c. specialized ability

5. ***Notwithstanding*** her parents' lack of interest, Sylvie became an excellent concert pianist.
   a. because of
   b. in spite of
   c. an example of

6. Professional athletes take part in ***intense*** training sessions, in which they work extremely hard.
   a. serious
   b. weak
   c. modern

7. Training for the Olympics requires an ***enormous*** amount of work; athletes who want to compete must work extremely hard.
   a. very common
   b. very unusual
   c. very large

8. Some people think their abilities have ***limitations***, but with encouragement they can perform much better than expected.
   a. possibilities
   b. certainties
   c. boundaries

9. A newspaper reporter ***quoted*** Thomas Alva Edison as saying, "Genius is one percent inspiration and ninety-nine percent perspiration."
   a. used exactly the same words as
   b. used completely different words than
   c. changed the meaning of words used by

10. ***Persistence*** is needed in order to succeed. You may fail several times before you get what you want.
   a. continuing a difficult activity
   b. ending a difficult activity
   c. succeeding in a difficult activity

11. Children with a special ***capacity*** for music learn to play musical instruments easily.
   a. chance
   b. ability
   c. room

12. My friend and his soccer coach are ***incompatible***. They are always arguing.
   a. too different to work together
   b. almost exactly the same
   c. related in some way

B The words below are also from the lecture. Read their definitions and the example phrases or sentences.

DNA *n* TECHNICAL deoxyribonucleic acid; an acid that carries genetic information in a cell

ease /iz/ *n* the quality of doing something easily or of being done easily: *Randy learns new languages* ***with ease***. | *I was surprised by the ease with which I had gotten reservations.*

gifted /ˈgɪftɪd/ *adj* having the natural ability to do something very well: *a gifted poet*

inherit /ɪnˈhɛrɪt/ *v* to get a quality, type of behavior, appearance, etc. from one of your parents: *Tony inherited his father's nose.*

training /ˈtreɪnɪŋ/ *n* the process of teaching or being taught skills for a particular job: *Did you have any training on the computer?*

world-class /ˌwɚld ˈklæs◂/ *adj* among the best in the world: *a world-class tennis player*

C Use a dictionary to check the pronunciation of the new words in Parts A and B.

Taking Better Notes

Noting Processes

In lectures, it's common for the speaker to describe a *process*. A process is a series of steps you take to reach a goal. It is used to give instructions or demonstrations (for example, in chemistry experiments) or explanations of procedures (for example, how diamonds are mined). When listening to an explanation of a process, you can increase your understanding by remembering two points:

- All the steps in the process have a logical order.
- Each step has a boundary, and often there is a clear boundary marker between steps.

Typical words and phrases used to show boundaries are:

First, second, third, etc.	After (that)	When
To start / begin with	Next	The final / last step
The first step	Then	Finally
Once this is completed	Afterward	

Read the explanation of the movie-making process below. Underline the words and phrases that show step boundaries.

> The first step in making a movie is to find a property, which is the story that the movie will be based on. Once the property has been selected, the script can be prepared. This can be a very time-consuming process. However, after the script has been written, the director can choose the cast. This involves finding the actors and actresses who can do a good job in this particular film. Once this step has been completed, filming can begin. Then the final step involves editing the film.

When taking notes on a lecture that includes a process, it can be helpful to list and number each step in the process. For example, the steps for making a movie can be listed and numbered as follows.

MAKING A MOVIE

1. find property—i.e., the story
2. prep. script
3. choose cast—i.e., actors & actresses
4. start filming
5. edit film

List the steps in a process you know well (for example, making tea or buying a used car.) Then work with a partner. Student A, explain the process, using words and phrases to show the different steps. Student B, take notes. Compare the notes with the list. Then change roles.

When you listen to a lecture, try to note the steps in any process that you hear.

Listening to the Lecture

Before You Learn

You will hear a lecture about the making of genius. Write two topics you think the speaker might discuss.

1. ______________________________

2. ______________________________

Listening for Main Ideas

A Close your book. Listen to the lecture and take notes.

B Use your notes to complete the statements below. Circle a, b, or c.

1. __________ support the idea that practice is important.
   a. Historical increases in performance
   b. Olympic records from ancient Greece
   c. Changes in athletic equipment

2. __________ also supports the idea that practice is important.
   a. The strong connection between diet and athletic performance
   b. The weak connection among intelligence, memory, and specific skills
   c. The effect of specialized knowledge

3. Along with practice, __________ also contribute to skill development.
   a. innate talent, general intelligence, and education
   b. diet, exercise, and sleep
   c. personality, motivation, and social support

4. To become an exceptional performer, most people must practice for __________ years.
   a. five
   b. eight
   c. ten

5. ____________ may be the most important sign that a child is gifted.
   a. An early desire to practice
   b. Ease of learning
   c. Incompatibility with the parents

6. According to the speaker, ____________ cause exceptional skill development.
   a. external factors, such as parental support,
   b. innate abilities, such as general intelligence,
   c. both external factors and innate abilities

Listening for Details

A **Close your book. Listen to the lecture again. Add supporting details to your notes and correct any mistakes.**

B **Use your notes to decide if the statements below are true or false. Write T (true) or F (false). Correct the false statements.**

_____ 1. Some people thought Wolfgang Amadeus Mozart had magical powers.

_____ 2. Expert chess players have better general memory skills than most people.

_____ 3. Self-confidence, persistence, and competitiveness play an important role in successful learning.

_____ 4. Mozart had been playing music for ten years before writing his first original masterpiece.

_____ 5. Expert musicians often show signs of greatness by the age of five.

_____ 6. About 15 percent of our personality characteristics and intelligence are genetically determined.

_____ 7. Working memory capacity is an inherited trait.

_____ 8. Ease of learning may indicate a child is gifted.

Using Your Notes

A **At the end of the lecture, the speaker summarizes the process of becoming highly skilled. The steps are listed below. Work with a partner. Use your notes to number the steps so that they are in the correct order. Compare answers as a class.**

_____ The child gains higher levels of skill.

_____ The child's motivation and social support create a long-term commitment to practice.

_____ Personality characteristics are nurtured by the parents.

_____ The person is born with certain personality characteristics.

_____ Long-term intensive practice (that is, around ten years) results in extremely high levels of skill.

_____ The child shows an interest in some area.

_____ The parents support the child's interest.

B **Look at the Note-Taking Tips below. Did you use any of them when you took notes? Which were most helpful? How can you improve your notes the next time you listen to a lecture?**

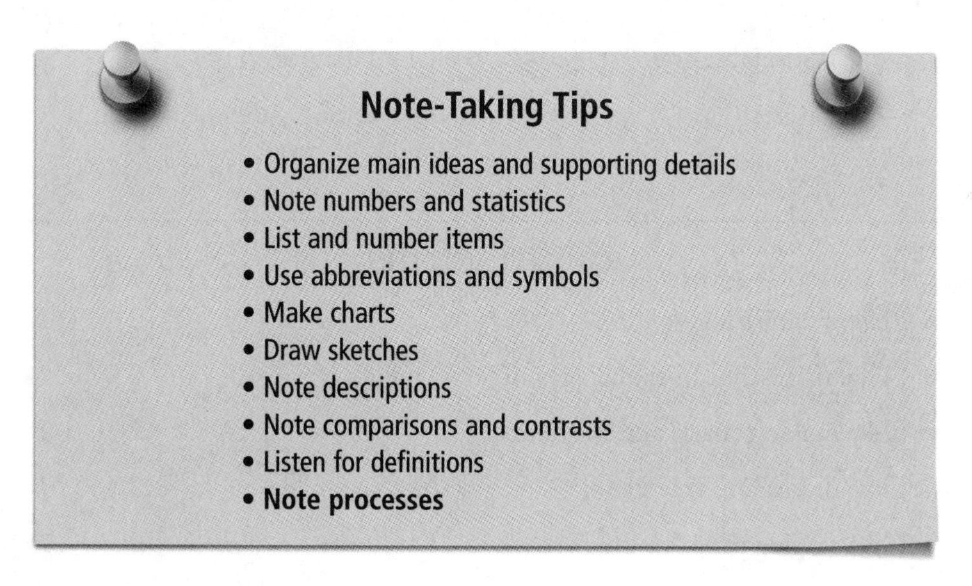

C **Rewrite or revise your notes so that the organization is clear. If you need to, listen to the lecture again.**

D **Use your notes to write a summary of the lecture.**

Projects

1. Imagine you are giving advice to a young person who wants to become a professional musician. Rank the pieces of advice below from 1 (most important) to 7 (least important). Compare and discuss your choices in a small group.

    _____ Study with a well-known teacher.

    _____ Talk to many professional musicians.

    _____ Practice extensively.

    _____ Perform in public frequently.

    _____ Make friends with other young people who want to be musicians.

    _____ Buy a high-quality musical instrument.

    _____ Attend many concerts.

2. Many people define *intelligence* as the ability to solve problems, think logically, and understand complex ideas. However, recent work in cognitive science and psychology has suggested that there are several types of intelligence, or multiple intelligences. Read the statements in the questionnaire. Circle the number that best describes you. Use the scale below.

    4 Strongly agree

    3 Agree

    2 Disagree

    1 Strongly disagree

QUESTIONNAIRE

a. I like memorizing words.	*4*	*3*	*2*	*1*
b. I like the teacher to explain grammar to me.	*4*	*3*	*2*	*1*
c. I like making charts and diagrams.	*4*	*3*	*2*	*1*
d. I like drama and role plays.	*4*	*3*	*2*	*1*
e. I like singing songs in English.	*4*	*3*	*2*	*1*
f. I like group and pair interaction.	*4*	*3*	*2*	*1*
g. I like self-reflection through journal writing.	*4*	*3*	*2*	*1*

Each lettered statement in the questionnaire corresponds to the type of intelligence below.

a = linguistic intelligence (ability to speak, write, or solve word problems)
b = logical-mathematical intelligence (ability to use numbers and logic or understand grammar rules)
c = spatial intelligence (ability to draw or use maps)
d = bodily-kinesthetic intelligence (athletic skill or ability to pronounce a language)
e = musical intelligence (ability to use music and produce the intonation of a language)
f = interpersonal intelligence (ability to talk and communicate with other people)
g = intrapersonal intelligence (ability to use language to analyze oneself)

The number you circled indicates your preference for the corresponding type of intelligence:

4	High preference	*2*	Moderately low preference
3	Moderately high preference	*1*	Low preference

For example, if you circled *4* for statement **a**, you strongly prefer to use linguistic intelligence, and if you circled *1* for statement **b**, you do not like to use logical-mathematical intelligence.

Do you think the correspondences correctly indicate your preferences? Discuss your answers in small groups.

3. Conduct library or Internet research on someone you consider a genius. Try to discover what factors contributed to the person's success. Give a five-minute report on that person to your classmates.

UNIT 11

Sociology

The New Global Superculture

Topic Preview

Work in small groups. Discuss the questions below.

1. What do think the expression *global superculture* means?
2. What symbols, products, or ideas represent a global superculture?
3. Do you agree or disagree with the following statements? Write A (agree) or D (disagree). Compare and explain your answers.

_____ The world is becoming a smaller place.

_____ Individual cultural traditions will eventually disappear.

_____ The media have a strong influence on the global superculture.

_____ Most people don't care about cultural traditions.

_____ People today are accepting more ideas from other cultures.

Vocabulary Preview

A The boldfaced words below are from a lecture about a global superculture. Read the sentences and the definitions that follow. Match each sentence with the correct definition of the boldfaced word.

_____ **1.** Some societies have a very ***homogeneous*** population. Almost everybody has the same appearance and belief system.

_____ **2.** The influence of some cultural traditions is ***diminishing***. One day, these traditions may disappear completely.

_____ **3.** Advertising is the most effective way of selling ***commodities***, such as food and clothes, worldwide.

_____ **4.** The Internet ***disseminates*** news and ideas around the world very quickly.

_____ **5.** The speaker ***highlighted*** the problems existing in today's society. Then she gave several examples.

_____ **6.** It is ***inevitable*** that people's lifestyles will become increasingly similar as the world becomes smaller.

_____ **7.** In big cities like New York, lifestyles are ***converging*** as immigrants introduce foods, languages, and other elements of their home cultures.

_____ **8.** In some parts of the world, there is ***prejudice*** against people because of their race, nationality, religion, or political beliefs.

_____ **9.** Frank is fascinated by politics; in particular, he's interested in how ***ideologies*** differ from culture to culture.

_____ **10.** Although Irene couldn't speak Spanish, she ***conveyed*** her meaning successfully by using body language and gestures.

_____ **11.** Travel can give us great ***insight*** into foreign cultures.

_____ **12.** We need to ***preserve*** cultural traditions that are in danger of disappearing.

a. consisting of the same parts or members
b. stop from being destroyed or changed
c. knowledge; understanding
d. coming together from different places
e. communicated
f. certain to happen; unavoidable
g. set of beliefs or ideas
h. spreads information or ideas
i. becoming smaller or less important
j. products that are bought or sold
k. unfair dislike based on race, religion, etc.
l. emphasized; made noticeable

B **The words below are also from the lecture. Read their definitions and the example phrases or sentences.**

aesthetic /ɛsˈθɛt̬ɪk, ɪs-/ *adj* relating to beauty and the study of beauty: *an aesthetic point of view*–**aesthetically** *adj*

diversity /dəˈvɚsɪt̬i, daɪ-/ *n* a range of different people, ideas, or things; VARIETY: [+ **of**] *It's natural that there is a diversity of opinions in the organization.*

emerge /ɪˈmɚdʒ/ *v* to begin to be known or noticed: *Marlena Fischer is emerging as a top fundraiser for the charity.*

fad /fæd/ *n* something that someone likes or does for a short time, or that is fashionable for a short time: *a fad for big baggy T-shirts*

materialism /məˈtɪriəˌlɪzəm/ *n* DISSAPROVING the belief that getting money and possessions is the most important thing in life

unprecedented /ʌnˈprɛsəˌdɛntɪd/ *adj* never having happened before, or never having happened so much: *The Steelers won an unprecedented four Super Bowls in six years.*

C **Use a dictionary to check the pronunciation of the new words in Parts A and B.**

Taking Better Notes

Noting Examples

When giving lectures, speakers often provide examples to clarify or make their points more interesting and real. The words and phrases below are used to signal examples.

. . . for instance . . .
. . . for example . . .
such as . . .
An example of this is . . .
Just look at . . .
. . . as an example

One way to take notes that include examples is to list them underneath the point they exemplify. Another way is to list them next to the point.

Look at the lecture excerpt and example student notes below.

> . . . The phrase "unity in diversity" describes a situation where people are united by a common world view, yet individual cultural traditions are given more and more respect. As a result, these individual cultures survive, even flourish. For instance, Mexicans and Americans may live side by side and follow many of their own traditions, but the great majority will have similar values, such as a belief in human rights and education for all, the need to eliminate prejudice, and so on. And they'll probably follow similar fashions; for example, most probably own computers or cell phones, watch the same television shows, eat fast food, enjoy similar sports, and have the same heroes. They may even begin to share and enjoy each other's traditions . . .

UNITY IN DIVERSITY— common world view, but
individ. cults survive
— e.g., Mex, U.S.
Common Beliefs
— human rights
— educ. for all
— stop prejudice
Common Fashions
— e.g., computers, cell phones, TV, fast food,
sports heroes

Work with a partner. Student A, explain how one aspect of your culture has changed (for example, customs, dress). Give examples wherever possible, and try to use different words and phrases to signal examples. Student B, take notes. Compare the notes with the explanation. Then change roles.

When you listen to the lecture, try to include examples in your notes.

Listening to the Lecture

Before You Listen

You will hear a lecture about a global superculture. Cross out the three topics you think the speaker is least likely to mention.

1. How ideas spread around the world
2. World-famous sports cars
3. How to do business in foreign countries
4. Why people's lifestyles are becoming increasingly similar
5. How the media promote celebrities
6. The world's best-loved foods

Listening for Main Ideas

A **Close your book. Listen to the lecture and take notes.**

B **Use your notes to complete the sentences below. Check (✓) a, b, or c.**

1. The first part of the lecture focuses on ____________ of the new global superculture.

   _____ **a.** causes

   _____ **b.** effects

   _____ **c.** characteristics

2. The second part of the lecture focuses on ____________ the new global superculture.

   _____ **a.** research about

   _____ **b.** history of

   _____ **c.** disadvantages of

3. According to the speaker, ____________ have contributed most to the development of a global superculture.

   _____ **a.** air travel, the media, and English

   _____ **b.** advertising, politics, and technology

   _____ **c.** fads, fashions, and pop music

4. According to the speaker, the main advantage of the new global superculture is ___________.

   _____ **a.** increased unity

   _____ **b.** higher standards of living

   _____ **c.** better governments

5. According to the speaker, the main disadvantage of the new global superculture is ___________.

   _____ **a.** increased prejudice

   _____ **b.** environmental problems

   _____ **c.** loss of cultural diversity

Listening for Details

A **Close your book. Listen to the lecture again. Add supporting details to your notes and correct any mistakes.**

B **Use your notes to answer the questions below. Compare your answers in small groups.**

1. According to the speaker, what is the best measure of cultural diversity?

   ____

2. What two types of revolution did the airplane cause?

   ____

3. What fads and fashions have become international phenomena?

   ____

4. Why do many movies and TV shows have universal appeal?

   ____

5. How has advertising caused people's habits and lifestyles to converge?

   ____

6. How have political circumstances influenced the global superculture?

   ____

7. How has immigration influenced the global superculture?

   ____

8. Where do the Ainu, the Chipaya, and the Penan come from?

   ____

Using Your Notes

A **Work with a partner. Exchange notes. Try to find examples of the following in your partner's notes:**

1. Products that have spread globally
2. Products that American commercials advertise
3. Food from other countries that Americans eat
4. Pop stars or groups that the media have promoted
5. Aspects of their culture immigrants bring into their new communities

Discuss how to make the examples in your notes clearer.

B **Check your notes against the Note-Taking Tips below. Did you use any of the tips when you took notes? Which were most helpful? How can you improve your notes the next time you listen to a lecture?**

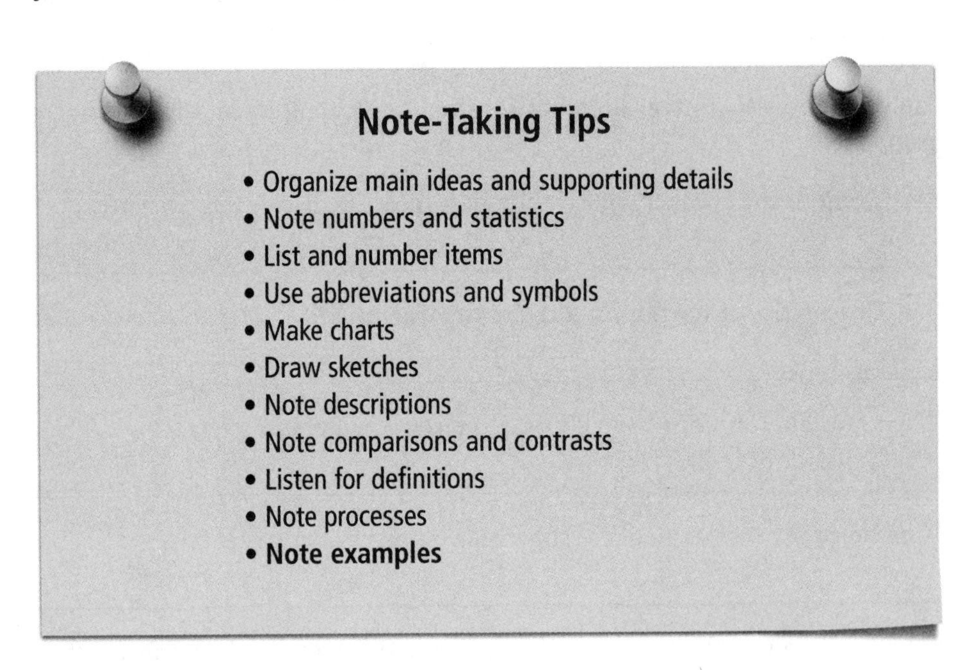

C **Work in small groups. As a group, use your notes to orally reconstruct the lecture, or describe it in detail.**

D **Rewrite or revise your notes so that the organization is clear. If you need to, listen to the lecture again.**

Projects

1. Bring an item (or picture of an item) to class that you think illustrates the idea of global culture. In small groups, explain why you think that item is a good example.
2. The excerpt below is about Survival International. Read the excerpt. Then discuss the questions on page 86 in small groups.

Survival International

Survival International is a worldwide organization supporting tribal peoples. It stands for their right to decide their own future and helps them protect their lands, lives, and human rights. Over the last thirty years, Survival International has developed imaginative ways to support tribal peoples' rights. In over half our cases they have brought positive results, saving lives today and bringing lasting benefits for tomorrow. This work can take many forms.

Organizations: In many countries, Survival supports tribal peoples' own organizations which have recovered land, made alliances, and refused to let their way of life be destroyed. Survival's funding of Aboriginal-run land councils in Australia, for instance, has helped these people win back control of their lives.

Media: Survival draws media attention to tribal peoples. Through articles, radio and television interviews, and advertising, it exposes the crimes committed against tribes, and governments and companies face criticism that threatens their international status.

Education: Survival believes that the most effective force for lasting change is widespread public concern, which can only come through knowledge and education. Survival conferences and educational resources—books, magazines, exhibitions, slideshows, films, and tapes—reach children and adults in over eighty-five countries. These influence public opinion and have received unprecedented praise from tribal peoples.

Money: Survival finds money for self-help and emergency projects. Small sums can bring great change. For example, Survival supporters raised over $2,000 for emergency medical work with the Yanomami people.

Demonstrations: Survival members hold regular and peaceful demonstrations at embassies and company headquarters in many countries—a silent protest at the violation of tribal peoples' rights. This tactic has proved very effective in shaming governments and influencing public opinion. A three-year embassy vigil helped in getting Yanomami land rights recognized.

Law: Survival advises on the drafting of laws concerning tribal peoples and provides legal advice in specific cases. Survival lawyers helped the Barabaig in Tanzania and Masai in Kenya in the fight for justice. Only when governments respect international law and human rights conventions will the future of tribal peoples be secure.

For more information, contact:
Survival International
6 Charterhouse Buildings
London EC1M 7ET UK
www.survival-international.org

a. What ways of supporting and protecting tribal cultures are mentioned?
b. Which way do you think is most effective? Why?
c. Which way do you think is least effective? Why?
d. Can you think of any other ways to support or protect tribal cultures? If so, what are they?

3. Prepare a five-minute presentation about your favorite cultural tradition for your classmates. Explain why you like it and how you would feel if it were to disappear.

UNIT 12

Computer Science

Computer Security

Topic Preview

Work in small groups. Discuss the questions below.

1. Look at the picture. What do you think the boys are doing?

2. Rank the following statements from 1 (least serious problem) to 3 (most serious problem).

_____ "I can buy things for free by getting other people's credit card numbers from the Internet."

_____ "I break into companies' computer systems, but I never do any damage. I just do it for the challenge."

_____ "I found a way to read other people's e-mail. I don't do anything but read it, so I don't really think that it's wrong."

Compare your answers. Should any of these actions be considered crimes? If so, which one(s)? Why?

Vocabulary Preview

A The boldfaced words below are from a lecture about computer security. Read each sentence. Circle the letter of the word or phrase that is closest in meaning to the boldfaced word.

1. Computer criminals can ***access*** private information by illegally entering a computer system.
   - a. discover and use
   - b. forget and abandon
   - c. discuss and understand

2. If you ***scramble*** an electronic message, most people won't be able to understand it.
   - a. send electronic signals
   - b. make electronic signals stronger
   - c. mix electronic signals

3. Although we don't know what will happen with computer crime in the future, we can imagine a few different ***scenarios***.
   - a. computer criminals
   - b. possible situations
   - c. new types of technology

4. Computer criminals try to ***cover up*** their crimes to avoid punishment.
   - a. leave
   - b. hide
   - c. report

5. Many computer criminals are not caught because it is very difficult to ***detect*** the theft of computer information.
   - a. discuss
   - b. protect
   - c. discover

6. Banks use computer networks to ***transfer*** huge amounts of money from one location to another every day.
   - a. steal
   - b. move
   - c. record

7. We can get large amounts of information ***via*** the Internet.
   - a. in spite of
   - b. by way of
   - c. away from

8. The ***transmission*** of information occurs every time we send an e-mail message or make a phone call.
   a. process of sending a signal
   b. process of changing systems
   c. process of printing a message

9. If one ***route*** into a computer system is blocked, computer criminals will search for another.
   a. piece of secret information
   b. type of computer crime
   c. way from one place to another

10. A ***colleague*** from the office had her credit card number stolen by a computer criminal.
    a. someone you work with
    b. someone who buys things
    c. someone who breaks the law

11. If they can't break into a computer system the first time they try, many computer criminals ***persist*** until they find a way to enter.
    a. stop working
    b. continue to try
    c. find a new job

12. The system administrators work hard to maintain the ***integrity*** of the company's computer systems.
    a. completeness
    b. size
    c. low cost

B **The words below are also from the lecture. Read their definitions and the example phrases or sentences.**

encrypt /ɪn'krɪpt/ *v* to change the form of computer information so that it cannot be read by people who are not supposed to see it–**encryption** /ɪn'krɪpʃən/ *n*

hacker /'hækɚ/ *n* INFORMAL someone who uses computers a lot, especially in order to secretly use or change the information in another person's computer system–**hacking** *n*

impersonate /ɪm'pɚsəˌneɪt/ *v* to pretend to be someone by copying his/her appearance, voice, etc. in order to deceive people: *They were arrested for impersonating police officers.*

modem /'moʊdəm/ *n* a piece of electronic equipment that allows information from one computer to be sent along telephone wires to another computer

software /'sɔftˌwɛr/ *n* a set of programs (= instructions) that you put into a computer when you want it to do a particular job: *word processing software*

virus /'vaɪrəs/ *n* a set of instructions secretly put into a computer that can destroy information stored in it

C **Use a dictionary to check the pronunciation of the new words in Parts A and B.**

Taking Better Notes

Noting Causes and Effects

When giving lectures, especially in the social and natural sciences, a speaker may discuss the causes or reasons for an event. The speaker may also discuss the results of the event or solutions to a problem. Listening for signals for cause-and-effect patterns can help you to understand the connection between different events, attitudes, beliefs, and behaviors.

The words, phrases, and questions below signal causes:

X is caused by Y	There are two causes / reasons...
X causes Y	The first cause of X is...

The following words, phrases, and questions signal effects:

If X happens, then...	Therefore...
The effect of X is...	Thus...
As a result...	Consequently...

One way to take notes about causes and effects is to list each cause or effect under the event or problem. Look at the example below.

COMPUTER REVOLUTION

3 Causes

— need for info. by govt. & researchers

— competition bet. countries

— tech. advances

3 Results

— spread of computers to public

— data transformed—written to digital

— creation of Internet

Work with a partner. Student A, list reasons why people use the Internet. Student B, take notes. Then change roles. Student B, list the effects of the Internet on people's lives. Student A, take notes. Compare and discuss your notes.

When you listen to a lecture, try to note the causes and effects of computer crime, and also the possible solutions.

Listening to the Lecture

Before You Listen

You will hear a lecture about computer security. Check two topics you think the speaker might discuss.

_____ **1.** Effective passwords

_____ **2.** Computer viruses

_____ **3.** Internet shopping

_____ **4.** The best computer equipment

_____ **5.** Security software

_____ **6.** E-mail

Listening for Main Ideas

A **Close your book. Listen to the lecture and take notes.**

B **Use your notes to complete the outline below.**

I. Reasons for computer crime

A. ______________________________

B. ______________________________

C. ______________________________

II. Effects of computer crime

A. On companies and/or governments

1. ______________________________

B. On individuals

1. ______________________________

2. ______________________________

III. Possible solutions

A. ______________________________

B. ______________________________

C. ______________________________

D. ______________________________

E. ______________________________

F. ______________________________

Listening for Details

A **Close your book. Listen to the lecture again. Add supporting details to your notes and correct any mistakes.**

B **Use your notes to decide if the statements below are true or false. Write T (true) or F (false). Correct the false statements. Compare your answers in small groups.**

_____ **1.** About 50 percent of companies that are online have experienced computer crime.

_____ **2.** More than $400 billion is transferred by the U.S. banking system every day.

_____ 3. Many computer criminals are motivated by financial gain.

_____ 4. Computer viruses have not affected government computer systems.

_____ 5. The courts' attitude toward computer crime has changed little in recent years.

_____ 6. A firewall stands between the Internet and a company's intranet.

_____ 7. A word chosen from a large dictionary is an effective password.

_____ 8. Access-control software limits people's access to information and operations.

_____ 9. Encryption software scrambles data so that hackers cannot understand it.

_____ 10. Audit trails tell computer users about attempts to hack into their computer systems.

Using Your Notes

A Work with a partner. Exchange notes. Take turns using your partner's notes to explain the following reasons, effects, and solutions.

1. Reasons for computer crime
   - a. sensitivity of information
   - b. financial gain
   - c. exciting challenge
2. Effects of computer crime on companies/governments
   - a. shut down computers
   - b. financial loss
   - c. work stoppage
3. Effects of computer crime on individuals
   - a. stolen credit card numbers
   - b. impersonation

4. Solutions to problem of computer crime
   a. courts
   b. firewalls
   c. passwords
   d. access-control software
   e. encryption software
   f. audit trails

Discuss how to make the causes, effects, and solutions in your notes clearer.

B **Check your notes against the Note-Taking Tips below. Did you use any of the tips when you took notes? Which were most helpful? How can you improve your notes the next time you listen to a lecture?**

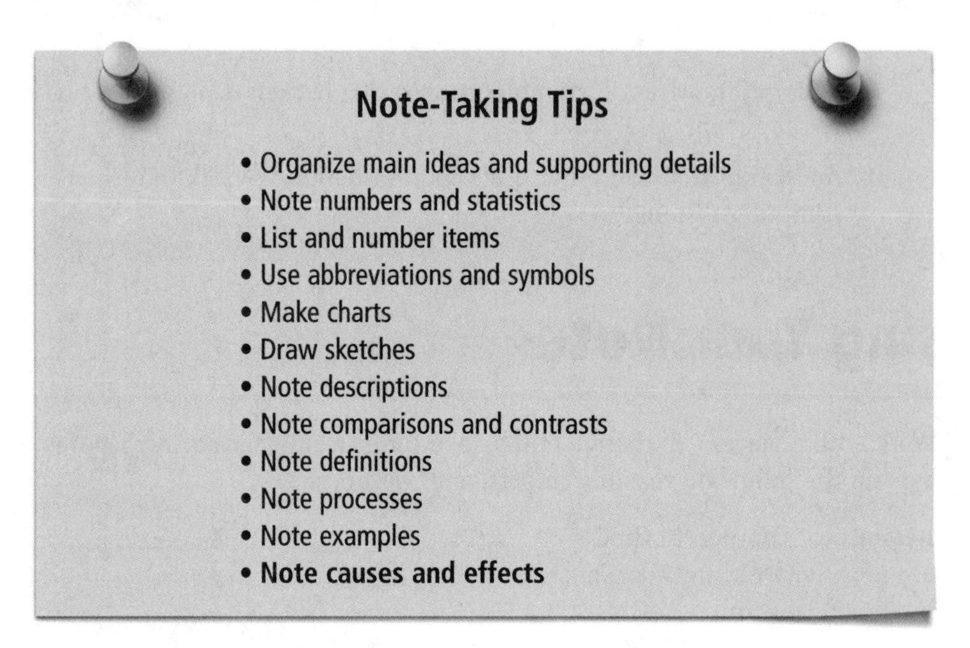

C **Rewrite or revise your notes so that the organization is clear. If you need to, listen to the lecture again.**

D **Use your notes to write a summary of the lecture.**

Projects

1. Read the article. Then discuss the questions on page 95.

Privacy in the Computer Age

Most people would agree that their lives have been positively affected by the Internet and e-mail. The Internet allows us to access large amounts of information on nearly any topic quickly and cheaply. E-mail allows us to communicate with friends, family, and colleagues almost instantly even when they are on another continent. However, a question on many people's minds concerns privacy. Does a company or government agency have the right to keep a record of the sites you visit on the Internet? Does your employer have the right to read your e-mail messages?

Democratic societies create large zones of privacy for individuals by limiting the power of public and private authorities to look into anyone's personal matters. Although privacy is still a very important value, the computer age has brought a new debate over privacy rights. Computer systems have made it easy for companies and governments to collect, store, and process data. This results in three potentially dangerous effects. First, organizations can collect far more personal information than ever before. Second, they can exchange the data with other organizations quickly and easily. Finally, they can use the information in ways that individuals do not know about and cannot control.

In North America and some European countries, traditional rules regarding privacy have been extended to cover computerized information practices. The concern for individual rights to privacy has resulted in three guidelines. First, individuals should know how any organization is using their personal data files. Second, rules for sharing personal data should be set and then made public. Third, everyone should have the right to inspect, correct, and challenge information in their personal files. Although these guidelines are a good beginning, finding the correct balance between the rights of organizations to collect and use personal data and individual rights will be a long process.

a. What are three potentially dangerous effects of modern computer systems?
b. What guidelines have some countries adopted to protect individual rights?
c. Do you agree with the guidelines? Why or why not?

2. Work in small groups. Make a questionnaire about computer use and security. Write at least five questions. (For example: *How often do you buy things on the Internet? What kinds of items have you purchased?*) Give the questionnaire to at least three people. Discuss and summarize your findings as a group. Report your findings to the class.

3. Find an article about computer privacy or computer crime in the library or on the Internet. Read the article and write a one-paragraph summary. Share it with your classmates.

Appendix A: Academic Word List

Numbers indicate the sublist of the Academic Word List (for example, *abandon* and its family members are in Sublist 8). Sublist 1 contains the most frequent words in the list, and Sublist 10 contains the least frequent.

abandon	8	approach	1	chart	8
abstract	6	appropriate	2	chemical	7
academy	5	approximate	4	circumstance	3
access	4	arbitrary	8	cite	6
accommodate	9	area	1	civil	4
accompany	8	aspect	2	clarify	8
accumulate	8	assemble	10	classic	7
accurate	6	assess	1	clause	5
achieve	2	assign	6	code	4
acknowledge	6	assist	2	coherent	9
acquire	2	assume	1	coincide	9
adapt	7	assure	9	collapse	10
adequate	4	attach	6	colleague	10
adjacent	10	attain	9	commence	9
adjust	5	attitude	4	comment	3
administrate	2	attribute	4	commission	2
adult	7	author	6	commit	4
advocate	7	authority	1	commodity	8
affect	2	automate	8	communicate	4
aggregate	6	available	1	community	2
aid	7	aware	5	compatible	9
albeit	10	behalf	9	compensate	3
allocate	6	benefit	1	compile	10
alter	5	bias	8	complement	8
alternative	3	bond	6	complex	2
ambiguous	8	brief	6	component	3
amend	5	bulk	9	compound	5
analogy	9	capable	6	comprehensive	7
analyze	1	capacity	5	comprise	7
annual	4	category	2	compute	2
anticipate	9	cease	9	conceive	10
apparent	4	challenge	5	concentrate	4
append	8	channel	7	concept	1
appreciate	8	chapter	2	conclude	2

concurrent	9	crucial	8	drama	8
conduct	2	culture	2	duration	9
confer	4	currency	8	dynamic	7
confine	9	cycle	4	economy	1
confirm	7	data	1	edit	6
conflict	5	debate	4	element	2
conform	8	decade	7	eliminate	7
consent	3	decline	5	emerge	4
consequent	2	deduce	3	emphasis	3
considerable	3	define	1	empirical	7
consist	1	definite	7	enable	5
constant	3	demonstrate	3	encounter	10
constitute	1	denote	8	energy	5
constrain	3	deny	7	enforce	5
construct	2	depress	10	enhance	6
consult	5	derive	1	enormous	10
consume	2	design	2	ensure	3
contact	5	despite	4	entity	5
contemporary	8	detect	8	environment	1
context	1	deviate	8	equate	2
contract	1	device	9	equip	7
contradict	8	devote	9	equivalent	5
contrary	7	differentiate	7	erode	9
contrast	4	dimension	4	error	4
contribute	3	diminish	9	establish	1
controversy	9	discrete	5	estate	6
convene	3	discriminate	6	estimate	1
converse	9	displace	8	ethic	9
convert	7	display	6	ethnic	4
convince	10	dispose	7	evaluate	2
cooperate	6	distinct	2	eventual	8
coordinate	3	distort	9	evident	1
core	3	distribute	1	evolve	5
corporate	3	diverse	6	exceed	6
correspond	3	document	3	exclude	3
couple	7	domain	6	exhibit	8
create	1	domestic	4	expand	5
credit	2	dominate	3	expert	6
criteria	3	draft	5	explicit	6

exploit	8	hypothesis	4	integral	9
export	1	identical	7	integrate	4
expose	5	identify	1	integrity	10
external	5	ideology	7	intelligence	6
extract	7	ignorance	6	intense	8
facilitate	5	illustrate	3	interact	3
factor	1	image	5	intermediate	9
feature	2	immigrate	3	internal	4
federal	6	impact	2	interpret	1
fee	6	implement	4	interval	6
file	7	implicate	4	intervene	7
final	2	implicit	8	intrinsic	10
finance	1	imply	3	invest	2
finite	7	impose	4	investigate	4
flexible	6	incentive	6	invoke	10
fluctuate	8	incidence	6	involve	1
focus	2	incline	10	isolate	7
format	9	income	1	issue	1
formula	1	incorporate	6	item	2
forthcoming	10	index	6	job	4
foundation	7	indicate	1	journal	2
found	9	individual	1	justify	3
framework	3	induce	8	label	4
function	1	inevitable	8	labor	1
fund	3	infer	7	layer	3
fundamental	5	infrastructure	8	lecture	6
furthermore	6	inherent	9	legal	1
gender	6	inhibit	6	legislate	1
generate	5	initial	3	levy	10
generation	5	initiate	6	liberal	5
globe	7	injure	2	license	5
goal	4	innovate	7	likewise	10
grade	7	input	6	link	3
grant	4	insert	7	locate	3
guarantee	7	insight	9	logic	5
guideline	8	inspect	8	maintain	2
hence	4	instance	3	major	1
hierarchy	7	institute	2	manipulate	8
highlight	8	instruct	6	manual	9

margin	5	ongoing	10	primary	2
mature	9	option	4	prime	5
maximize	3	orient	5	principal	4
mechanism	4	outcome	3	principle	1
media	7	output	4	prior	4
mediate	9	overall	4	priority	7
medical	5	overlap	9	proceed	1
medium	9	overseas	6	process	1
mental	5	panel	10	professional	4
method	1	paradigm	7	prohibit	7
migrate	6	paragraph	8	project	4
military	9	parallel	4	promote	4
minimal	9	parameter	4	proportion	3
minimize	8	participate	2	prospect	8
minimum	6	partner	3	protocol	9
ministry	6	passive	9	psychology	5
minor	3	perceive	2	publication	7
mode	7	percent	1	publish	3
modify	5	period	1	purchase	2
monitor	5	persist	10	pursue	5
motive	6	perspective	5	qualitative	9
mutual	9	phase	4	quote	7
negate	3	phenomenon	7	radical	8
network	5	philosophy	3	random	8
neutral	6	physical	3	range	2
nevertheless	6	plus	8	ratio	5
nonetheless	10	policy	1	rational	6
norm	9	portion	9	react	3
normal	2	pose	10	recover	6
notion	5	positive	2	refine	9
notwithstanding	10	potential	2	regime	4
nuclear	8	practitioner	8	region	2
objective	5	precede	6	register	3
obtain	2	precise	5	regulate	2
obvious	4	predict	4	reinforce	8
occupy	4	predominant	8	reject	5
occur	1	preliminary	9	relax	9
odd	10	presume	6	release	7
offset	8	previous	2	relevant	2

Word	Sublist
reluctance	10
rely	3
remove	3
require	1
research	1
reside	2
resolve	4
resource	2
respond	1
restore	8
restrain	9
restrict	2
retain	4
reveal	6
revenue	5
reverse	7
revise	8
revolution	9
rigid	9
role	1
route	9
scenario	9
schedule	8
scheme	3
scope	6
section	1
sector	1
secure	2
seek	2
select	2
sequence	3
series	4
sex	3
shift	3
significant	1
similar	1
simulate	7
site	2
so-called	10
sole	7
somewhat	7
source	1
specific	1
specify	3
sphere	9
stable	5
statistic	4
status	4
straightforward	10
strategy	2
stress	4
structure	1
style	5
submit	7
subordinate	9
subsequent	4
subsidy	6
substitute	5
successor	7
sufficient	3
sum	4
summary	4
supplement	9
survey	2
survive	7
suspend	9
sustain	5
symbol	5
tape	6
target	5
task	3
team	9
technical	3
technique	3
technology	3
temporary	9
tense	8
terminate	8
text	2
theme	8
theory	1
thereby	8
thesis	7
topic	7
trace	6
tradition	2
transfer	2
transform	6
transit	5
transmit	7
transport	6
trend	5
trigger	9
ultimate	7
undergo	10
underlie	6
undertake	4
uniform	8
unify	9
unique	7
utilize	6
valid	3
vary	1
vehicle	8
version	5
via	8
violate	9
virtual	8
visible	7
vision	9
visual	8
volume	3
voluntary	7
welfare	5
whereas	5
whereby	10
widespread	8

Appendix B: Affix Charts

Learning the meanings of affixes can help you identify unfamiliar words you read or hear. A *prefix* is a letter or group of letters added to the beginning of a word. It usually changes the meaning. A *suffix* is a letter or group of letters at the end of a word. It usually changes the part of speech.

The charts below contain common prefixes and suffixes. Refer to the chart as you use this book.

Prefixes

Meaning	Prefixes	Examples
not, without	a-, ab-, il-, im-, in-, ir-, un-	atypical, abnormal illegal, impossible, inconvenient, irregular, unfair
opposed to, against	anti-	antisocial, antiseptic
with, together	co-, col-, com-, con-, cor-	coexist, collect, commune, connect, correlate
give something the opposite quality	de-	decriminalize
not, remove	dis-	disapprove, disarm
no longer, former	ex-	ex-wife, ex-president
out, from	ex-	export, exit
outside, beyond	extra-	extracurricular, extraordinary
in, into	im-, in-	import, incoming
between, among	inter-	international
later than, after	post-	postgraduate
in favor of	pro-	pro-education
half, partly	semi-	semicircle, semi-literate
under, below, less important	sub-	subway, submarine, subordinate
larger, greater, stronger	super-	supermarket, supervisor

Suffixes

Meaning	Suffixes	Examples
having the quality of, capable of (*adj*)	-able, -ible	comfortable, responsible
relating to (*adj*)	-al, -ial	professional, ceremonial
the act, state, or quality of (*n*)	-ance, -ence, -ancy, -ency	performance, intelligence conservancy, competency
the act, state, or result of (*n*)	-ation, -tion, -ion	examination, selection, facilitation
someone who does a particular thing (*n*)	-ar, -er, -or, -ist	beggar, photographer, editor, psychologist
full of (*adj*)	-ful	beautiful, harmful, fearful
give something a particular quality (*v*)	-ify, -ize	clarify, modernize
the quality of (*n*)	-ility	affordability, responsibility, humility
a political or religious belief system	-ism	atheism, capitalism
relating to (or someone who has) a political or religious belief (*adj*, *n*)	-ist	Buddhist, socialist
having a particular quality (*adj*)	-ious, -ive, -ous,	mysterious, creative, dangerous
a particular quality (*n*)	-ity	popularity, creativity
without (*adj*)	-less	careless, worthless
in a particular way (*adj*)	-ly	briefly, fluently
conditions that result from something (*n*)	-ment	government, development
quality of (*n*)	-ness	happiness, seriousness